Was ever book containing such vile matter
So fairly bound? O, that deceit should dwell
In such a gorgeous palace!
— William Shakespeare, *Romeo and Juliet. Act iii. Sc. 2.*
British dramatist & poet (1564–1616)

You Won't Get Fooled Again

You Won't Get Fooled Again:

More Than 101 Brilliant Ways to Bust *Any* Bald-Faced Liar (Even If the Liar is Lying Beside You!)

Conner O'Seanery

Illustrated by Steve Reed

St. Thomas

Published in 2006 by
The FingerTip Press
14 Chestnut Street, Suite 104
St. Thomas, ON, Canada N5R 2A7
www.tipsdigest.com

Library and Archives Canada Cataloguing in Publication

O'Seanery, Conner, 1967-

You won't get fooled again : more than 101 brilliant ways to bust any bald-faced liar (even if the liar is lying beside you!) / Conner O'Seanery ; illustrated by Steve Reed.

Includes bibliographical references and index.

ISBN-10: 0-9739277-0-4
ISBN-13: 978-0-9739277-0-2

1. Truthfulness and falsehood--Humor. I. Reed, Steve, 1979- II. Title.
BJ1421.O83 2006 177'.30207 C2006-902570-3

Editor: Bobbie Jo Reid
Cover and Book Design: 1106 Design
Research Assistant: Michele Halle

First Edition
Printed and bound in Canada
10 9 8 7 6 5 4 3 2 1

For Carlo Collodi. No strings attached.

A lie can travel halfway around the world
while the truth is putting on its shoes.
— Mark Twain
American humorist, novelist, short story author
& wit (1835–1910)

Contents

List of TipBits

Chapter 4: The Mind-Blowing Lies of Bald-Faced Liars

Chapter 5: Technology to the Rescue?

Chapter 6: Even More Brilliant Ways to Bust Any Bald-Faced Liar

Man seems to be an animal whose capacity for lies
is only equaled by his credulity;
it does no good to let battalions of cats out of bags,
to produce whole harems of naked facts,
people eat the same three meals daily deception,
and are always ready to turn with fury upon
the purveyors of bagless cats and facts undraped ...
— John Dos Passos
American novelist, poet, playwright & painter (1896–1970)

Introduction

People everywhere are doing it. Some people are doing it dozens of times a day. Most have it done to them once every eight minutes. Sometimes it's done face-to-face. Other times it's done behind the back. It's done to complete strangers. It's done to people sharing the same bed. It's done out of love. It's done out of pure malice.

People everywhere are lying through their teeth.

A Lie by Any Other Name

Men•dac•i•ty (n.) The quality of being mendacious. To be mendacious is to be characterized by deception that is not intended to genuinely mislead. *Riiiiiiight.*

Mendacity is a universal phenomenon. It crosses the lines of gender, race, religion and culture. It transcends the sands of time. If you subscribe to the Garden of Eden tale, you know we lied in our earliest incarnation:

"Apple?" Eve did sayeth unto God. "What apple?"

TipBit: An Apple a Day Keeps Paradise at Bay

The notion that Eve got busy with a McIntosh – and lost us paradise in the process – is deeply ingrained in both Christian and secular culture. But before you storm the local market to upset the apple cart, stop and consider this: The precise Bible passage (Gen. 3:3) reads, "The fruit of the tree that is in the middle of the garden." Note how the word "apple" is nowhere to be seen. For all we know, Eve could have noshed on an orange or a grapefruit or, for that matter, a tomato. Except tomatoes don't grow on trees.

Even if you're a Darwinian at heart, it doesn't take a bold leap of imagination to picture Neanderthal man dipping his hand into the "brontosaurus jar" behind his fellow cave-dwellers' backs, then grunting out a quick excuse to cover his hairy backside:

"Me? Steal food? No, I was down at the 7-11 picking up a pack of Virginia Slims."

Baby, we haven't come such a long way. But why expect any different? Deception comes naturally to all creation. Birds fake injury to lead predators away from nesting young. Octopi walk on two tentacles, strutting all gnarly on the sea floor, pretending to be algae (or Jessica Alba's hairdo in *Sin City*'s promo shots) to escape their enemies. Wolves dress in sheep's clothing.

Nature's deceivers are rewarded by longer life — which means more opportunities to reproduce. And while lying may no longer be necessary to procreate (though it can help), the spinning of a late-night, alcohol-soaked yarn has certainly preserved the quality of many a man's life.

A Lie by Any Other Name

Spin a Yarn *(v.)* A longwinded story used to embellish one's adventures. Derived from the nautical expression for weaving hemp into rope — a tedious freakin' task at the best of times. Just like listening to your husband's high-school "glory-days" stories.

So, a dubious thread of lies is woven through our existence, binding us together in this elaborate fabrication called life. *You Won't Get Fooled Again: More Than 101 Brilliant Ways to Bust Any Bald-Faced Liar (Even If the Liar is Lying Beside You!)* will help unravel the biggest blanket of b.s., equipping you to catch the 200 fibs and full-blown fabrications tossed your way *every single day.* (Hopefully, not all are tossed by your partner, or else we really need to talk.)

The brilliant tips and TipBits bursting from the pages of this ready reference digest will give any reader a competitive edge in innumerable situations. Slip it into your pocket when you go shopping for that used car (sorry, *previously enjoyed* car). Tuck it in the desk drawer at the office before you grill the intern with the suspiciously impressive résumé. Keep it on the coffee table in the den for the President's next State of the Union address or Prime Minister's Throne Speech. And — for sure — stash it in the bedside table for the next time you breathlessly ask your spouse, "How was that?"

A Lie by Any Other Name

Du•plic•i•tous *(adj.)* Marked by deliberate deceptiveness in behavior or speech, especially by pretending one set of feelings and acting under the influence of another.

You Won't Get Fooled Again will get you one step closer to that grand goal of life: The Truth.

Hey, would I lie to you?

— Conner O' Seanery,
Address Withheld By Request, 2006

Vulgar Word Alert!

As a service to our faithful readers around the world — and to the governments whose arbitrary fiddling with customs duties could erase our already slender profit margin — The FingerTip Press reserves this space in every *Tipping Points Digest* for Vulgar Word Alerts.

While no digest published by The FingerTip Press would dare touch the Holy Trinity of swear words with a ten-foot typewriter ribbon, certain works may contain potentially offensive words, sentences or paragraphs (or entire chapters if they refer in any way to the National Hockey League's '04–'05 season). Our Vulgar Word Alert! service is designed to safeguard you, the reader, and your loved ones from potential trauma. Think of this service as the literary equivalent of the FCC's five-second delay for live-television broadcasts.

You Won't Get Fooled Again features salty or suggestive language on the following pages: 21, 36, 41, 48, 55, 80, and 102.

Parents of impressionable ankle-biters are advised to either:

1. Strike the offensive word(s) using black, indelible marker;
2. Tear out the offensive page(s) and shred along with your bank statements and the unpublished novel you've been working on for eight years; or
3. Stash the digest in the same place you hide your "artistic" late-night material.

Remember: Forewarned is forearmed.

The Men, Women and Children of The FingerTip Press

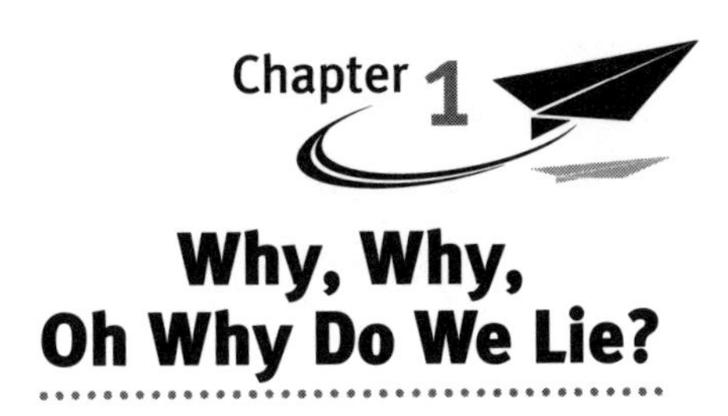

Why, Why, Oh Why Do We Lie?

A lifetime of relationships is inconceivable without deception.
—David Nyberg
Author of *The Varnished Truth: Truth Telling and Deceiving in Ordinary Life*

People sure are strange, huh? Take Ricky, my second cousin with the unibrow and the accounting credentials. Not long ago, he padded his résumé to snag a plum office job with a plum corner office. He then told his co-workers at the same plum office he couldn't make a staff party due to a prior commitment when, in truth, he'd sooner have shaved his unibrow with a cheese grater than hang out with them during his off time. A year later, in a panic to avoid a ten-year stretch in San Quentin, he told federal investigators he didn't cook the books for his plum employers. Honest!

Ricky lied every step of the way. His story is instructive — and just one of billions floating around this naked planet of ours. In truth, there are as many reasons for why people lie as there are people wandering aimlessly about the earth. And in truth once again, our lives are very likely better for it. Our love lives, especially.

TipBit: Classify Your Lies!

In *Lies! Lies!! Lies!!!: The Psychology of Deceit,* Charles V. Ford, M.D. provides a classification of lying, adapted from the *Encyclopedia of Aberrations: A Psychiatric Handbook.* Here's another adaptation of that adaptation (with apologies to Dr. Ford and the psychiatric profession) from a guy's perspective:

Type of Lie	Motive
Benign and Salutary lies	To make oneself less of a sniveling dweeb
Hysterical Lies	To say, "Hey, look at me! Look at meeeeee!!"
Defensive Lies	To bail oneself out of the doghouse
Compensatory Lies	To get oneself a little somethin' somethin'
Malicious Lies	To ruin others and pillage their possessions
Gossip	To kill an hour before quittin' time
Implied Lies	To say anything out loud
"Love Intoxication" Lies	To invite her over after last call
Pathological Lies	To live and breathe

Deception is the grease that makes the world of relationships spin smoothly. Imagine, for a second, that you had to speak the God's-honest truth to your partner for one day. Twenty-four hours of the truth, the whole truth and nothing but the truth. If you can't imagine it, rent a copy of *Liar Liar* from your favorite video store. This 1997 Jim Carrey vehicle features a lawyer, of all people, rendered incapable of lying thanks to a potent birthday wish from his son. If you think love's tough now, try loving with brutal honesty.

TipBit: Fibs, Lies and Videotape

In a study conducted in 2002, psychologist Robert Feldman of the University of Massachusetts Amherst secretly videotaped 121 college students who were asked to talk with a stranger. Later, the students were asked to analyze their tapes and keep tabs on their fibs.

Incredibly, 60 percent admitted to lying at least once during just 10 minutes of conversation. The group averaged three fabrications in that time period, ranging from intentional exaggeration to full-blown hoodwinking.

A Lie by Any Other Name

Hood•wink *(tr.v.)* To blindfold, hide or deceive by presenting a false appearance. To influence by slyness.

TipBit: "Hi, I'm a Serial Liar"

The Josephson Institute of Ethics in Marina Del Ray, California, conducts biannual surveys of thousands of middle school, high school and college students. The majority score themselves highly with respect to ethics and personal character, 'cause six figures of personal debt hasn't yet opened their eyes to the wealth-generating opportunities a lack of ethics brings.

Ominously, however, about three-quarters of the kids also admit to being "serial liars." Most fib to save a buck or score a job — and most display an irritating, "watcha gonna do about it, huh?" arrogance that they'll never be busted.

Why Johnny is Cool

Research doesn't lie: The most popular adolescents are most proficient at fooling their peers. Better liars also tend to find jobs more readily and attract members of the opposite sex into relationships more readily.

It's not just our words that reek of deception. The sweaty stench of artifice permeates virtually every aspect of our being. Consider the Hair-Club-for-Men client who adorns his scalp with an atrocious "piece" or the eighteen-year-old model who opts for breast enhancement. Consider the millions of North Americans who fund their lifestyles with credit cards, mortgaging the future to cast a false image of abundance *right now.* Creating fictions seems to be hard-wired into the species.

A Lie by Any Other Name

Ar•ti•fice ***(n.)*** An artful strategy. False or insincere behavior, used especially in social situations.

"I'M NOT ONLY THE PRESIDENT... I'M ALSO A CLIENT!"

As much as we cast out fictions for strangers, we keep the best for ourselves, lubricating our passage through life with prevarications. It's only natural this icky lube slops onto our partners from time to time. But if we're not careful, the slippery goop can build up and eject a soul mate out of our lives faster than a bar of Ivory from a soapy hand.

A Lie by Any Other Name

Pre•var•i•cate *(intr.v.)*

To walk crookedly, with feet spread apart.

To deviate from the truth, or evade it altogether.

CAUTION: SLIPPERY WHEN DECEIVED.

So, let's dip our heads in the goop and see what we can learn (besides not to dip our heads in goop). Who knows? The more we understand about why our loved ones can't lie straight in bed, the less inclined we might be to chuck them out on the street at the first sign of deception.

Men Should be Banished to Mars

TipBit: From the Mouths of Babes

According to Jack Trimarco, former FBI profiler and host of Court TV's *Fake Out,* men tend to lie to make themselves feel better. Women, on the other hand, tend to lie to make others feel better. (Jack mustn't have tuned into recent shows like *Desperate Housewives,* 'cause I don't see a whole lotta lying to make others feel better on the screen.) Trimarco says everyone has the initial instinct to lie to avoid getting in trouble. We learned it when we were kids. If we lied and got away with something, we weren't punished and — let's face it — we seek pleasure and avoid pain. Great! One more thing to blame on our parents.

The verdict is in. Men and women lie for different reasons, and have different definitions of what even constitutes a lie. Here's a favorite quote that yields brilliant insight into how a guy views a lie:

> *That's not a lie, it's a terminological inexactitude.*
> — Alexander Haig
> Former U.S. Secretary of State

Of course, Haig was famous for his *Haigisms.* (He also served as Richard Nixon's Chief of Staff during the Watergate crisis and was long touted as a possible candidate for *Deep Throat,* the covert source Woodward and Bernstein used to break the scandal.) But his scatological comment on lying throws the gender difference into stark relief:

- ❖ Men tend to view lies as a misstatement of facts.
- ❖ Women tend to view lies as intentional untruths that hurt someone.

This key difference opens up a whole whack of interesting dynamics between the sexes (as if there weren't already enough interesting dynamics between the sexes):

- ❖ A disturbingly high percentage of men believe not mentioning something — say, a sexual dalliance during their off time — doesn't qualify as a lie. Their rationale? No statement = no misstatement = no lie.
- ❖ Men tend to view the relationship game as bloodthirsty competition — a sort of *Blind Date* meets *Gladiator,* set to the *Top Gun* soundtrack. They self-aggrandize (translation: they lie their faces off) in order to squash puny rivals and cart home the spoils of war (which, dear ladies, is you).
- ❖ Women lie more readily in social situations because they are more sensitive. *Sniff* ... tissue, please. They reason it's better to boost a person's ego with a little white lie than destroy them with the truth. (Wow, talk about a foreign concept.)
- ❖ Women tend to be dishonest in their private lives, usually to protect their children or their friends. *Borrrrring* ...

A Lie by Any Other Name

White Lie *(n.)* A harmless fib, usually viewed as pardonable because it's motivated by kindness or a desire to avoid hurting someone's feelings. White denotes purity, but you already knew that.

These gender-induced differences have consequences. Women's lies, for example, aren't terribly reckless or sexy. Men's lies, on the other hand, can be wickedly creative (as you'll learn in the following chapters). In fact, lies born of men can border on fully developed philosophical systems, complete with airtight internal logic, external followers and tax-exempt status from the government.

TipBit: The Truth About Sexual Partners

A U.S. study surveyed the sexual history of over 200 unmarried, heterosexual college students aged 18 to 25. One group filled in questionnaires after being told researchers might view their responses. A second group completed the survey anonymously. A third group was wired with electrodes and told they were being attached to a lie detector machine (actually, no such machine was used in the test).

Women who thought their responses might be read admitted an average of 2.6 sexual partners, compared with 3.4 partners for those who thought their answers were anonymous. But those who thought they would be busted by the lie detector reported an average of 4.4 partners.

The men's answers didn't vary significantly. Those attached to the "lie detector" reported an average of 4.0 partners, compared with 3.7 for men who thought their answers would be read.

When it comes to fibs, another crucial difference between the sexes relates to their orientation. Of the fibs, that is:

- Men tell more self-oriented lies, ones designed to gain an advantage for the liar.
- Women tell other-oriented lies, ones designed to help someone else (usually the recipient of the lie).

The B.S. Meter is Off the Scale

A typical conversation between two guys contains about eight times as many self-oriented lies as it does whoppers about other people.

A Lie by Any Other Name

Whop•per *(n.)* An exceptionally large or remarkable untruth.

Who's the Most (and Least) Likely to Lie?

O.K., we know everyone lies. We also know men and women stretch the truth in different directions with different intentions. No huge surprise. The most important question when it comes to busting those bald-faced liars is this: Are there any ways to avoid latching onto a bald-faced liar in the first place?

Surprisingly, there are. And surprisingly, the people most (and least) likely to lie aren't who you'd think:

- Cutting-edge research by cutting-edge researchers reveals that those annoying, overly sociable extroverts are slightly more likely to lie than the rest of us conniving malcontents. Certain personality and physical traits, most notably self-confidence and physical attractiveness, have also been linked to how well an individual lies when the pressure's on. Better looking? Better liar!

- The people least likely to lie are those who score high on psychological scales of responsibility and those with meaningful same-sex friendships. Close behind these folks comes a third group of straight shooters: Depressed people.

Yep, depressed people. In *Lies! Lies!! Lies!!!,* Dr. Charles Ford suggests individuals who wallow in the mire of depression seldom deceive other people — or are deceived themselves. He attributes this to their ability to perceive and describe reality with greater accuracy than damned optimists. Seems Dr. Ford is onto something; other researchers such as UCLA's Dr. Shelley Taylor agree that a certain level of self-delusion is the key to good mental health.

TipBit: I Admit It ... Not!

Think for a second: When's the last time you heard someone say, "I'm sorry, I lied to you,"? In *The Post-Truth Era: Dishonesty and Deception in Contemporary Life*, Ralph Keyes notes that this kind of admission is as rare today as hash browns and toast on an Atkins-dieter's breakfast plate.

The trend is due to the stigma carried by a known fabulist. Instead of risking the label of liar, people will claim to "massage" or "sweeten" the truth, or tell "the truth improved." Keyes spotlights Donald Trump — the King of Brand — as a shining example. When *Trump: The Art of the Deal* came out, the Brand King claimed that 200,000 copies had been printed, that five interviews had been lined up with *The Today Show,* and that the *New York* magazine issue featuring the book's excerpt was its biggest seller ever.

Pshaw! Keyes points out that, in reality, only 150,000 copies were in print, only two *Today Show* interviews took place, and *New York's* sales figures weren't yet available when Trump made the comment. Why the exaggeration? All part of Trump's doctrine of "truthful hyperbole," as touted in *Art of the Deal.*

A Lie by Any Other Name

Hy•per•bo•le *(n.)* To exceed. To employ extravagant exaggeration (and comb-overs?).

When searching for someone with whom to share the passage through life (or when shopping around for a spare to replace a partner who's gone flat), it seems we face a tough choice. Pick the attractive, well-adjusted guys and gals and risk ending up with a pathological liar who looks fantastic at the beach. Or pick the dark, brooding types who spend every long weekend alone

DOES THIS TOGA MAKE ME LOOK FAT?

in the bedroom with the shades drawn, but have a much firmer grip on reality.

Hmm, I'd say it's too close to call.

What's It All About, Alfie?

In the final analysis, it probably doesn't matter what kind of mate we pick. Perhaps it's enough to know every one of them will lie. That's what people do. Whether it's for personal gain, to avoid hurting others, to make ourselves more likable, to avoid the negative consequences of rash actions, or to cover the manure we've already spread, mendacity is a universal condition. We lie so easily and so often because it works.

So, let's accept that which we cannot change, continue deluding ourselves, hoist in the tips that follow, and get busy busting those bald-faced liars!

TipBit: Is Lying Ever the Right Thing to Do?

Great question. Let's consult the historical record:

Truly, to tell lies is not honorable;
but when the truth entails tremendous ruin,
To speak dishonorably is pardonable.

—Sophocles, *Creusa*
Greek tragic dramatist (496 BC–406 BC)

Now, let's put Sophocles in context. How would you answer this question?

"Honey, does this toga make me look fat?"

Honest answer: Two-and-a-half millennia haven't changed a damn thing.

TipBit: So That's What Girls are Made of ...

A 2003 survey commissioned by *That's Life!* magazine polled 5,000 women in England, Wales, Scotland and Northern Ireland to gauge their level of deception toward their partners. The average age of respondents was 38. Caution: Some responses may be disturbing for younger men.

- ❖ Half the women polled said they would lie to their husbands or partners to preserve the relationship if they became pregnant by another man.
- ❖ 33% said they would stay with their husband if they found out he was a "secret transvestite."
- ❖ Only 17% would put up with their husband if he refused to wash. (Funny, coming from England and all, I'd have thought the women's tolerance for unwashed mates would be much higher ...)
- ❖ 83% admit to telling "big, life-changing lies," with 13% telling them frequently.
- ❖ Only 27% said they'd tell a man if he was useless in bed, but 36% would tell their friends every juicy detail.
- ❖ 54% would flatter a man if he asked about his looks, and only 46% would give the "brutal truth."
- ❖ 61% want their partners to be "brutally honest" if they ask them, "Do I look fat?" or "Do you think my best friend's attractive?" (Guys who respect

this wish do so at their extreme peril and are rejected by most life-insurance companies.)

- ❖ 49% would "kiss and tell" to the media for £25,000 ($44,000) if they had a one-night stand with a celebrity.
- ❖ 23% would allow their man to sleep with another woman for £50,000 ($88,000). (Hey guys, now's the time to check the balance of your 401(k)s and RRSPs!)
- ❖ 46% fake orgasms.
- ❖ 55% claim they are tired, have a headache, or feel sick to "get out of lovemaking."
- ❖ 30% have had an affair with a married man.
- ❖ 68% do not trust their partner.

TipBit: Does a Ring Mean Fewer Lies?

Many love-struck couples believe that marriage will inoculate them against deception. Research by Dr. Bella DePaulo, a psychology professor at the University of California, suggests otherwise.

Spouses routinely lie to each other in about 10% of their conversations, but that statistic captures only the minor fibs of everyday life. When it comes to big-ticket lies involving thorny issues like the betrayal of trust, the vast majority occur between people entrenched in the most intimate expression of relationships: marriage.

"You save your really big lies," says Dr. DePaulo, "for the person that you're closest to."

Oh, honey. And you say I never give you anything.

Mendacity is a system that we live in.
Liquor is one way out and death's the other.
— Tennessee Williams
American playwright (1911–1983)

Through all the lying days of my youth
I swayed my leaves and flowers in the sun;
Now I may wither into the truth.
— William Butler Yeats
Irish poet & playright (1865–1939)

Sign, Sign, Everywhere a Sign: Tips to Spot the Verbal Slips of Lying

Any fool can tell the truth, but it requires a man of some sense to know how to lie well.
—Samuel Butler
English composer, novelist & satiric author (1835 – 1902)

More than a great opening quote, Samuel Butler's words provide crucial insight into the subject of lying: To do it well takes some degree of intelligence.

The fool tells his wife he has to work late at the office, and then whisks his secretary to a seedy motel room and charges it to his credit card. A month later, the evidence of the tryst arrives with the Visa bill and he's got some quick explaining to do. Good luck with that, buddy. Odds are he'll be looking for a bachelor apartment before the next Visa bill arrives.

Lying takes effort. For most of us, it takes a lot of effort — most of the time. Sure, it's easy to tell a Greenpeace telemarketer you're on the way out the door when, in fact, you're dressed in your cozies and about to settle down for an hour of *The O.C.* Lying to a stranger over the phone is a cake walk, but what happens when that stranger is standing at your door? The task becomes harder. You're eye-to-eye now. Up close.

Substitute the stranger at the door for your nose-whistling soul mate, and lying becomes up close *and* personal. The degree of difficulty ratchets up. *Waaaay* up. So too does the effort it takes to not get caught. You'll see this person again, despite your best efforts. You'll have to remember your fable, and all its sordid details. Lying, for dummies, ain't so simple.

Truth be told, lying ain't so simple for smarty-pantses, either. And that's a good thing. Because it isn't so simple, most liars emit signs, leaks or "tells"—clues both subtle and obvious to betray their subterfuge.

A Lie by Any Other Name

Sub•ter•fuge *(n.)* Deception by artifice used to conceal or misrepresent the true nature of an activity.

TipBit: The Pantomime

I'm the anti-Christ, and you've got me in a vendetta kind of mood. Tell the angels in heaven that you had never seen evil so singularly personified as you did in the face of the man who killed you.

—Vincenzo Coccotti
All-around bad dude

In *True Romance,* Vincenzo Coccotti (Christopher Walken) interrogates Clifford Worley (Dennis Hopper) over the whereabouts of Worley's son, who's just pinched a suitcase of cocaine belonging to Coccotti's mob boss.

Coccotti, with classic passive-aggressive aplomb,

first explains how he learned the "pantomime" from his father, the world-heavyweight champion of Sicilian liars:

"There are seventeen different things a guy can do when he lies to give himself away. A guy's got seventeen pantomimes. A woman's got twenty ... [and] if you know them like you know your own face, they beat lie detectors all to hell."

An interrogation, he tells a battered and bruised Worley, is like a game of show and tell:

"You don't want to show me nothin', but you're telling me everything."

Interesting Grace Note: Coccotti's quest for the truth is aided by pre-*Sopranos* mob boss James Gandolfini, who gets medieval on Worley's poor arse.

Now, before you run off with the following tips and accuse your lover(s) of deception, here's a harsh dose of truth: There's no single sign or group of signs that prove beyond a shadow of a doubt that a person is lying. Dr. Paul Ekman, North America's leading authority on lying and author of *Telling Lies: Clues to Deceit in the Marketplace, Marriage and Politics*, echoes this sentiment:

"There are only signs that people are thinking more than you might think they would need to about their answer."

The challenge in busting a bamboozler is discerning the often infinitesimally small changes in speech, behavior and physical appearance that surface when someone addresses a topic untruthfully. In this chapter, we'll examine the verbal tics — those slips of the lip that can trip up a bald-faced liar.

A Lie by Any Other Name

Bam•boo•zle (*tr.v.*) To conceal one's true intentions from someone by an elaborate feint of good intentions.

Note: The tips that follow portray the liar as a guy. This is not to suggest that all liars are guys or all guys are liars (as you learned in Chapter One). It's merely a handy way for a lazy writer to avoid clunky, politically correct pronoun combinations like he/she, him/her, etc. If it's political correctness you're looking for, you've come to the wrong digest. And let's face it; a guy's self-oriented, self-destructive lies are far more entertaining than a gal's other-oriented, feel-good fibs.

Slips of the Lip: The Verbal Tics of Lying

Expansion & Contraction

A liar tends to expand contractions. "I didn't stay up all night surfing those websites" becomes "I *did not* stay up all night surfing those websites," with an indignant look thrown in for good measure. Or "I couldn't come to bed because I was busy reading The Bible" becomes "I *could not* come to bed because I was busy reading The Bible." A liar thinks his high-falutin' King's English will convince people he's telling the truth. But if that ain't the way he usually talks, somethin' ain't right. He could be hiding some dirty laundry — or dirty Internet habits.

TipBit: Listen Carefully

Using data collected from a text analysis program, Dr. James Pennebaker of the University of Texas and Dr. Dianne Berry of SMU determined there are certain language patterns that predict when someone is hiding the truth. Liars tend to use fewer first-person words such as "I" or "my" in both speech and writing. Emotional words like "hurt" and "angry" are also used less frequently, as are cognitive words such as "understand" or "realize." So, grab a tape recorder and let the interrogation begin.

B-b-b-bad to the Bone

A liar might stutter, stammer and otherwise wrap his tongue around his forehead. But it's impossible to know whether this is because he just nicked the Craftsman tools out of your garage (if he's your neighbor) or was dropped on his head as a baby (if he's any other guy you've ever known).

Pause and Insert Here

A liar may pause and insert odd, non-word sounds into his speech to fill the uncomfortable silence:

"Ah, I know I should have called, but, er, I couldn't tear myself from my, um, mother's side. Oh, she's been really sick lately and, um, and I ... duh."

Ah, er, um, oh and sometimes *duh* are a liar's vowels.

What's in a Name?

A liar might use pronouns instead of actual names, hoping to add a bit of emotional distance to his lie.
Of course, if he always dwells in a vapor of distraction, the lack of names might be par for the course.

Grunts and Groans

A liar might clear his throat often and make other strange, guttural noises — like an East German sausage tester the morning after a Jägermeister bender. Incidentally, these noises, if captured in stereophonic sound and released on compact disc, would sell better than anything William Shatner has ever recorded.

TipBit: Four Score and Five Drafts Ago

As far as speeches are concerned, Abraham Lincoln's Gettysburg Address ranks as one of the all-time best. The envy of stammering Toastmasters dropouts around the globe, Lincoln's speech is widely believed to have been drafted at the 11th hour during his train ride to Gettysburg — the 19th-century equivalent to an English major cranking out an A+ essay on Fitzgerald's use of symbolism in *The Great Gatsby* during the subway ride to NYU. As with most myths, however, the truth's much more mundane. Lincoln actually wrote multiple drafts of the address on White House stationery long before he indelibly stamped his words on the nation's conscience.

Let Me Qualify This

A liar might make judicious use of namsey-pamsey qualifiers such as "however," "sometimes," and "generally," stitching his fast-and-loose excuses with this limp, verbal pasta. Here's a scenario:

You're in the market for a previously enjoyed car. You locate a reputable dealership (excuse me while I laugh my glutes off) downtown and arrive to find a lot brimming with potential vehicles. A salesman approaches, slipping on a pair of Ray-Bans. He reminds you of your cousin, Albert; the one who's always calling up out of the blue to talk about the latest "make millions at home with no money down" scheme involving the sale of vitamins that, by weight and volume, are worth more than weapons-grade plutonium.

"Morning," the salesman says, "anything in particular you're looking for?"

You absently place your hand on your wallet and state your preferences. The salesman nods and says he has just the ticket. He leads you to a row of cars deep in the lot, stopping at an electric-orange, two-door compact about five years past its best-before date.

"Here's the perfect car for you," he says. "It's a peach."

You suppress an easy reference to the overripe quality of the "fruit" before you, and remind the salesman that this particular compact has been cited for such minor annoyances as a tendency to explode in rear-end collisions.

He nods again, flashing a smile. "You know, statistics sometimes get blown up out of proportion. [The salesman fails to notice his ironical use of "blown up" and continues without so much as a pause.] Sure, there were rumors of faulty gas tanks on this model, years ago. However, there was never any real proof. This baby's got 100,000 miles left on the engine and the body's decent."

"It's *my* body I'm concerned with," you reply. "It's got about forty years left on it and I'd like to wait until I'm dead before I'm cremated."

The salesman presses on, sunglasses glinting, cheesy grin undiminished. "Well, if anything hits this baby, generally speaking, the odds are you will be dead."

You exit stage left before he can start telling you about this great home-based vitamin business that would be perfect for a sharp and ambitious person like you.

Clumsy Is as Clumsy Does

A liar can be as clumsy with his words as former president Gerald Ford was with his footwork. Mistakes in grammar, verb tenses and other train-of-thought derailments might indicate deception. Or they might indicate he holds the current Office of President. It's just so damn hard to tell nowadays.

TipBit: A Poodle of Muddle

The French poodle is pure fiction. The breed comes in three varieties: standard; miniature; and toy. (Muddy, alas, is not a breed.) The French are nuts for the dogs, likely because "poodle" is such a treat to say with a contrived French accent.

A Trapped Rat

Once cornered, a liar will probably deny he's lying. He'll claim (with a nasally whine and a pounding fist) that he has no reason to lie. Uh-huh. You know better — he has *every* reason to lie.

Could You Repeat That?

A liar might repeat the question you just asked in order to buy time. Here's another scenario:

You and your husband are snuggling on the couch, late on a Friday night after the kids are tucked in bed. It's mid-November and just starting to snow. Nice fluffy flakes, the size of your fist. The glowing embers in the fireplace pop and hiss, soaking your domestic bliss with their thermal backwash.

You inhale, priming your lungs for a contented sigh, and the malodorous stench of pickled eggs b'yotch-slaps you upside da head. Your face scrunches as you glare through watering eyes at your husband, the filthy bastard. He sinks deeper into the couch.

"Did you just fart?" you ask.

"Did I just fart?" he replies, feigning shock. His brow furrows, like it does when he's trying to calculate an 8% tip at Red Robin, and his gaze darts about the living room floor.

"The dog left the room ten minutes ago, dillhole," you say.

"Ah, did I tell you, er, how great you look in that, um, sweater? Oh … duh."

Smooth Talker

Unlike the farting husband in the previous scenario, a liar might talk fast. And smooth. And convincingly. This means

PU

you'll need more tools in your toolbox. You'll need the tips featured in Chapter Three!

TipBit: All the Ham was Smoked, and the Bread was Fresh

In *No Cure for Cancer,* Denis Leary does a hilarious bit about Cass Elliot (Mama in The Mamas and the Papas) and her windpipe's untimely encounter with a ham sandwich. The bit's a bit callous, but there's no denying the popular misperception that poor ol' Mama succumbed to a Dagwood laced with pork.

In fact, the autopsy subsequently identified heart failure as the cause of Elliot's death, a complication of her obesity rather than her meal choice. The sandwich myth arose when her physician jumped the autopsy gun and offered the trendy "vomit-inhalation-after-choking-on-sandwich" explanation.

Personally, I think Porky Pig said it best when he said, "Th-th-th-th-th-that's all, folks."

Truth is beautiful, without doubt;
but so are lies.
— Ralph Waldo Emerson
American essayist & poet (1803 – 1882)

Movers and Shakers: Tips to Spot the Non-Verbal Signs of Deception

The cruelest lies are often told in silence.
—Robert Louis Stevenson
British writer, essayist, poet & novelist (1850 – 1894)

Mark Twain, whose wonderful quote stands alone on the opening pages of this digest, had lots to say on the subject of lying. If you'll permit, I'll dip into his expansive and incisive inkwell one more time, 'cause I couldn't put it any better in a month of Sunday rewrites:

> *Everybody lies … every day, every hour, awake, asleep, in his dreams, in his joy, in his mourning. If he keeps his tongue still his hands, his feet, his eyes, his attitude will convey deception.*

Props to Twain. If you haven't had a chance yet, pick up his books. All of them. Next to this digest, you'd be hard pressed to put anything better on your bookshelf.

Sorry … awkward fan digression and some shameless self-promotion. Twain's observation, however, cracks the nail on the noggin and sets up the tips featured in this chapter beautifully.

"A false face must hide what a false heart doth know,"

William Shakespeare once posited. Plundering the work of the greats aside, these men — acute observers of the human condition — recognized that the signs of deception manifest in far more than mere speech.

Fear, liar's remorse and even breathless excitement at the prospect of pulling off an audacious snow job can cause myriad changes inside a fibber's body ... changes that ripple outward and crest on the surface, providing unique "tells" or leaks. Some leaks are obvious to the naked eye; others are so imperceptible they require specialized training and advanced equipment to detect. In this chapter, we'll examine the naked-eye signs, the ones anyone can spot if they know what to look for. Ready? Let's shake it down!

A Lie by Any Other Name

Snow Job *(n.)* An attempt to deceive someone by using insincere claims or flattery. Derived from the ability of snow to obscure a person's vision and hide the appearance of objects on which it falls.

TipBit: The Signs of Primate Prevarication

As reported in *The Post-Truth Era,* Koko, the infamous "signing" gorilla, could b.s. with the best of them. After breaking a toy cat, Koko signed that a colleague of her trainer was responsible. When busted for eating crayons, she pretended to be using them as lipstick by signing "lip." When caught red-handed using chopsticks to poke holes in a screen, Koko signed "smoke mouth," a game she enjoyed playing with sticks. (An unsubstantiated rumor also has it that Koko, accused by forensic accountants of inflating the zoo's financial earnings by $11 billion, signed, "It's Scott Sullivan's fault.") When she knew the jig (with the chopsticks) was up, she signed, "Bad again. Koko bad again."

Note how the sign, "I'm sorry, I lied to you," wasn't forthcoming. No one, not even a gorilla, likes to be branded a liar.

The Naked-Eye, Non-Verbal Signs of Lying

Not-So-Lazy Eyes

In a worldwide study, scientists polled thousands of people from nearly 60 countries, asking "How can you tell when people are lying?" The number one response from America to Zimbabwe? *Liars avert their gaze.*

But caution is in order. How a person averts his gaze is crucial to understanding the underlying thought process:

- Does he look up and to the left (from your vantage point)? He's probably constructing an image or a situation. Hmm, could be a lie in the making.

- Does he look left, but with his eyes on the same level? He could be imagining a conversation he never had.

- To make this all the more complicated, looking right (again, from your vantage point) tends to indicate genuine recall of images/situations (if the gaze is upward) or sounds (with a level gaze).

And what if he glances down, you ask? Um, he's probably just checking his fly.

Face Off ... to the Side

Closely related to averting the gaze, a liar might be unable to show you his two-faced face. He may turn it away, indicating deception. Or that he's checking out the waitress in the short skirt serving the table next to yours.

Closed Hands; Closed Case

A liar might close his hands or interlock his fingers. Not sure if you knew this already, but open palms are a traditional sign of honesty. The habit comes from a time when two people would show their palms on meeting, indicating they weren't packing heat.

Cross to Bear False Witness

A liar may cross his arms, barrier-like, to fend off your inquisition. If he's a pasty-faced nancy-boy with arms like *al dente* spaghettini, he may need reinforcements and unconsciously place objects (like books, coffee cups, retaining walls, etc.) between him and you.

Happy Feet

A liar might tap his feet or wave his foot in the air if he's sitting with legs crossed. Depending on how long you've been grilling him, this could simply indicate an urgent need for the bathroom. Or an unrealized desire to dance the light fantastic.

Drink and Be Contrary

A liar tends to swallow more often than someone telling the truth. He'll also drink anything he can get his mitts on. There may, however, be another explanation for the heavy drinking, like his unrealized desire to dance the light fantastic.

Shweaty Balls

A liar may sweat more, which could make him adjust his clothing and scratch like a golfer with a 1 handicap.

A Stiff One

A liar may seem stiffer and use fewer hand gestures. Hmm, that's odd; most guys become stiffer when they ... sorry, that tip's just too yucky to complete.

Monkey's Uncle

A liar may perform hand-to-face grooming, frequently touching the face, ears and hair. That's *his* face, ears and hair, not yours. This trait may be employed by the chronically vain as well. It's also frequently used by men who haven't evolved that far from our simian cousins.

TipBit: You Got a Tell

Seinfeld elevated lying to an art form like no other television series. In a classic episode, Jerry asks Elaine how things are going with her latest boyfriend.

"Fine," Elaine replies emphatically, hand rising to scratch her cheek.

Jerry smirks. He knows she's lying.

Jerry interprets Elaine's hand-to-face gesture as a sign of mendacity. "It's a tell," he explains. "You got a tell."

Just like that, she's busted.

Handling Fees Included

A liar might handle objects: eyeglasses, pens, snifters of fine cognac, and — of course — the cookies in the cookie jar.

Blink 91

A liar tends to blink less frequently than someone telling the truth. Stone-cold psychopaths don't blink at all. If you're romantically involved with a psychopath, however, his lies probably aren't the highest item on your grocery list of relationship issues to work on.

Blink 364

A liar might blink more often than someone telling the truth. Yeah, I know, but no one said this would be easy.

Let Your Backbone Slide

A liar might shrug his shoulders, flipping his palms over in a palms-up fashion. While these are common traits among hip-hop artists and angst-filled tweens, it doesn't necessarily mean these groups harbor notorious liars. It must be noted, however, that anything they sing/say should be taken with a grain of salt (and few extra-strength Tylenol gelcaps).

Let Your Fingers Do the Pointing

A liar may do less finger pointing. Actually, since you're the one who suspects him of lying, it's you who's doing the finger pointing.

TipBit: Sometimes You Git the Bar; Sometimes the Bar Gits You

A persistent myth floats from tapa bar to tapa bar at the beginning of every summer. You've probably heard it: How the best course of action upon encountering a bear in the wild is to play dead.

Play dead? Good luck with that, pal. The way I figure it, anyone with enough presence of mind to lie perfectly still while getting the third degree by an 800-pound grizzly's snout wouldn't be stupid enough to get into the predicament in the first place. Want a better plan? Make sure you hike the Rockies with a buddy — preferably one you can feed an endless string of beers at weekend BBQs beforehand. Guaranteed those extra carbs will bog him down when Yogi appears around a bend in the trail and the flight instinct kicks in full blast. Remember: You don't have to outrun the bear ... just your buddy.

Shift Target Right

A liar may shift around a lot, leaning forward, resting his elbows on desks, shifting weight from foot to foot. Hmm, what witty prose can I add to expand on this tip? … Ah crap, I got nothin'.

The Incredible Shrinking Man

A liar might limit his physical expressions, and his arm and hand movements may seem oddly mechanical and directed toward his body. This indicates a desire to take up less space. Sprinting for the door represents the pinnacle of this desire.

Microexpressions

The emotions triggered by lying can cause changes in facial expressions so brief that most observers never notice. Dr. Paul Ekman has coined these split-second phenomena "microexpressions." He says these clues can be as important as the more obvious gestures and speech patterns in uncovering deception.

Timing's Off

The timing between a liar's gestures and words may appear off. Displays of emotion, if any, are delayed and may remain longer than they would naturally. If your boyfriend is acting like an extra in a poorly dubbed Jackie Chan chop-socky flick, then odds are something other than the truth is his motivation.

Flushed Cheek's a Leak

A liar's cheeks might flush. Put him through the grinder long enough and his commode'll be flushing next — right after he dumps in his shorts.

What a Sigh 'Tis There

A liar may sigh more often. So will a man utterly defeated by life (or an '04–'05 NHL fan, which is essentially the same thing).

Lip-Licking Liars

A liar may lick his lips more often. *Eeeww!* The only people permitted to lick their lips more often are supermodels and NBA MVPs whose names rhyme with Steve Nash. No exceptions.

Pucker Up

A liar might pucker and tighten his lips. *Eeeww*! See previous tip.

Joke's on You

A liar might use sarcasm and humor to deflect your suspicion. DO NOT BE FOOLED. Your partner isn't funny at the best of times.

TipBit: Twin (Sexual) Peaks

In the never-ending, multifaceted debate between the sexes regarding sex, no myth has saturated the populace more thoroughly than that which asserts men peak sexually in their late-teens while women, um, hit their rhythm in their mid-30s ... or beyond. Point of order, Mr. Chairman! The truth is, *both* sexes peak sexually in their late-teens.

Some experts attribute the misperception to cultural differences. Society places more pressure on women to repress their sexuality, so they tend to subvert their animal desires until they are older and more comfortable with their bodies. Now that you mention it, those *Girls Gone Wild* participants *do* look buttoned down.

Smile, You're Busted

A liar is more likely to smile or laugh at inappropriate times. Or, if he's using sarcasm and humor to deflect your suspicion, he could be one of those annoying types who laugh at their own jokes. Don't worry, there's a special place in Hell reserved for those people.

Puberty Revisited

A liar's voice may become more tense or high-pitched. If your methods for extracting the truth include a knee or other blunt object to the groin, the change in pitch could have a perfectly innocent explanation.

Skirting the Surface

A liar may skirt around the answer, never really addressing your suspicion head on. Kind of like every politician you know.

What, Me Lie?

A liar might phrase his answer in the form of a question, like he's looking for your reassurance. Here's a scenario:

You and your fiancé are packing the last of the luggage into the car for a Thanksgiving trip upstate to stay with your parents. A darker cloud of silence than normal looms over your man, whose only words in the past hour have been used to curse Samsonite and the horse the company rode in on. Your spider senses tell you something may be amiss.

With luggage stowed, you scamper into the front seat and tuck a manila folder crammed with lovely antiquing destinations downloaded off the Internet between the seat and the console. Your fiancé starts the car, revving the engine in the high 9000s before dropping the clutch. Once your head snaps upright again, you decide to find out if something's bothering him.

"Honey," you ask softly, "is everything all right?"

Amid grinding gears and strange mumbling, he doesn't respond.

You speak up. "Honey, you're excited to be taking this trip, right?"

He tosses you the look normally reserved for change-hustling street people. "Could I *be* anymore excited about spending Thanksgiving weekend antiquing with your parents?"

If the phrase and tone remind you of Chandler from *Friends,* your mate is probably bending the truth. And you probably watch too much TV.

TipBit: Cell Phones Explode onto the Market

Here's a scenario: You're in your SUV and running late for work. Five miles from the office, the "Low Fuel" light starts blinking on the console. You pull into the next gas station and start filling up, knowing you're going to be *really* late by the time you pump 500 gallons into your petroleum-pig-on-wheels. Ever resourceful, however, you grab your cell phone and autodial your assistant. You hear one ring before a blinding flash of light marks the end of your life.

The static charge emitted by your cell phone sparked a catastrophic explosion, right?

No way. This myth was doused during the first season of The Discovery Channel's *MythBusters.* Like all good fibs, however, it was supported by a bevy of details: widely circulated (and completely made-up) e-mails about cell-phone sparked explosions; warnings from cell-phone manufacturers; panicky signs at gas stations. But as Adam Savage and Jamie Hyneman proved on *MythBusters,* the fable has more creative spark than real spark.

Too bad. With today's prices, we need a convenient way to firebomb gas stations.

Temporizing For Liars

A liar might pause before he answers, taking extra time to frame a response in the dark corners of his mind before he commits it to speech. Here's another scenario:

You arrive home from the grocery store after a fruitless search for sun-dried tomatoes to find dirty dishes still piled in the sink and the carpet unvacuumed, despite your husband's assurance that he'd "get on them in a second" before you left. Friends will be arriving in less than an hour for the dinner party.

You find your husband in the living room, still watching *SportsCenter*, still wearing the faded NYU t-shirt with the oil stains, still glassy eyed and unshaven. You resist the urge to throw the jar of sun-dried tomatoes you don't have at him and simply stare, gaze set to London broil.

He notices your presence during the next commercial break and bolts upright, wide eyed, like a deer on a deserted stretch of highway hearing the whine of monster-truck tires approaching.

"You said you were going to take care of the dishes and the vacuuming," you say.

He swallows and nods, clicking off the TV. "Yes, yes I did, but …" His voice trails off.

The clock on the mantle tics off the seconds. *Tic. Tic. Tic.*

"But I …" The rank aroma of plodding thoughts, like burning ozone, fills the living room. "But I, uh …"

Tic. Tic. Tic.

You grab the clock and throw it instead.

NYU

Say Cheese

A liar's smile will usually look insincere. Remember how your mom used to say it's easier to smile than frown? Well, Momma was right! It takes only two muscles (the *zygomaticus major* muscles extending from the cheekbones to the corners of the lips) to paste one on your face. This also makes smiles easy to fake, so look for a lack of movement of the wrinkle lines around the eyes. A classic tell of a bald-faced liar. Or Botox injections.

Nasal Appraisal

A liar might touch his nose frequently. Many noted psychologists and mendacity experts commented on former president Bill Clinton's nasal manipulation during his testimony on his relationship with Monica Lewinsky. In fact, this habit has been reported in many cultures. It may be due to the fact that the nose contains erectile tissues that engorge when a person lies. If I'm not mistaken, that's a nose hard-on. Suddenly, *Pinocchio* never seemed so wrong.

Windows of the Soul

A liar will telegraph his true feelings through the upper face. Focus not on the mouth and chin — focus on the eyes. They are the windows of the soul.

Resist Self-Deception

According to renowned human-behavior expert David Lieberman, author of *Never Be Lied to Again: How to Get the Truth in 5 Minutes or Less in Any Conversation Or Situation*, one of the biggest obstacles to busting a bald-faced liar is our own self-deception. We want to believe someone is telling us the truth. Suppress this urge. With over 200 fibs and fabrications coming your way every day, your wishful thinking is letting some lying bastard get away with it.

The visionary lies to himself, the liar only to others.
— Friedrich Nietzsche
German philosopher (1844 – 1900)

The best liar is he who makes the
smallest amount of lying go the longest way.
— Samuel Butler

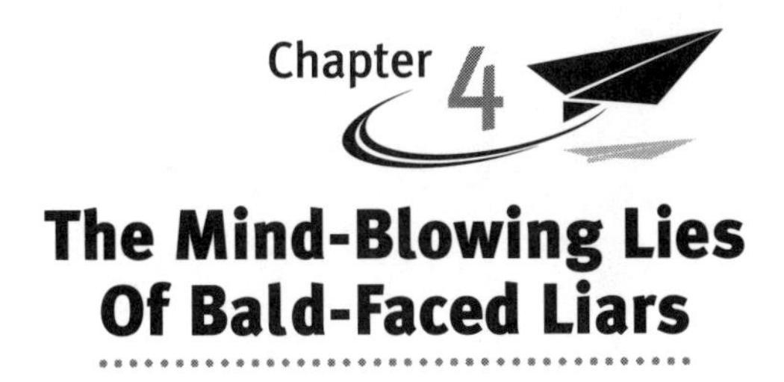

The Mind-Blowing Lies Of Bald-Faced Liars

I lied and I lied – and then I lied some more.
Jayson Blair, author of *Burning Down My Masters' House*
Former *New York Times* reporter

No book on busting liars would be complete without a choice selection of exposés from some of life's biggest b.s.'ers. These are the people who boggle our minds, confound our senses and stagger our imagination with the depth and depravity of their deceit. Choice selection, however, means *choice selection.*

You'll find no exposés of Bush Senior or Junior in this chapter. You'll find no Clinton or Chrétien, and no — I say again — no Nixon. Including politicians in a chapter devoted to mind-blowing liars would be too easy and too obvious, and lead to *waaaay* too many entries. This is a digest, after all — not a multi-volume *Encyclopedia Britannica.* You can read about the crooked ways of our elected officials to your heart's content in your favorite newspaper on a daily basis.

TipBit: NBC Announces a Fresh New Series for the Fall Lineup

Watch for a gritty new drama on NBC this fall. *CYA: Washington* follows the exploits of a tight-knit gang of Beltway insiders as they thread their own maze of lies, half-truths and double-breasted suits in the nation's capital.

Including politicians in a chapter devoted to mind-blowing liars would be too easy and too obvious, and lead to *waaaay* too many entries. This is a digest, after all — not a multi-volume *Encyclopedia Britannica*.

Rather than take the easy road, this chapter instead examines some of the most conniving lies told by men; men whose fabrications shook the very foundations of polite society. So much the better to learn from their truth trangressions. Each example of men-at-work-at-lying comes complete with a layman's psychoanalysis and a lesson for laymen, providing even more fuel to fight the prevarications coming your way. Some of the men highlighted below may be familiar; others obscure. But they all have one thing in common: They lied their freakin' faces off — and they got busted.

Most researchers agree that people lie most often about three things: Age, income and sex.

Baron Münchausen (1720 – 1797): Rider of Cannonballs

A German officer who served in the Russian army, Baron Münchausen's outlandish exploits were captured by Rudolph Erich Raspe in *Baron Münchausen's Narrative of His Marvellous Travels and Campaigns in Russia* in 1785. How outlandish are we talking here? Among other things, Münchausen claimed to have ridden a cannonball shot from a cannon, as well as a horse that had been sliced in two. The Baron's trippy tales were resurrected in the 1989 Terry Gilliam film, *The Adventures of Baron Münchausen.* Not very mind blowing, you say? Rent the movie tonight, drop a tab of acid, and then tell me it's not mind blowing. Hide the car keys and have fun!

A Layman's Psychoanalysis: The Baron's embellished stories were likely intended to get him great press coverage in his day — and a wee bit of immortality. Well, it worked. Here we are, over 200 years after his death, and we're still talking about him.

A Lesson for Laymen: Guys will lie tirelessly to boost their self-image and create a legacy that extends beyond the grave.

TipBit: Wasn't that a (Tea) Party

Everyone who's anyone has heard of the Boston Tea Party. And everyone who's anyone knows the incident was sparked when the damned Brits raised U.S. tea taxes, right?

Wrong. The raid on the ships in Boston Harbor was provoked when the British Parliament passed the Tea Act of 1773.

The Tea Act ... sounds harmless, doesn't it? Like an innocent play featuring stuffed animals and miniature cups and saucers. It wasn't. The act gave Britain's East India Company a monopoly on the import of tea into the colonies — and squeezed American tea companies out of the process. In protest, Samuel Adams and his band of merry men (which included John Hancock) trashed a few tons of East India's finest tea. The protest, however, had nothing to do with U.S. taxes being raised. Still, the affair rooted Sam Adams' place in history, and ultimately got his name on millions of beer bottles.

Charles Ponzi (1882–1949): Father of the "Ponzi Scheme"

A Ponzi scheme is one where initial investors — those who get in on the ground floor — are paid with money provided by later investors. It's a classic "robbing Peter to pay Paul" scam. All's well and fine until the pool of new investors dries up and the "pyramid" comes crashing down. It takes its name from the

International Reply Coupon (IRC) scheme hatched by Charles Ponzi in the 1920s.

What the hell's an IRC, you ask? These pre-paid postage slips are still available from post offices around the world. Say you're sending a letter to Canada from the U.S. and want the recipient to reply by mail. Being a courteous bastard, you'd like to include a stamp so the guy isn't out of pocket fifty cents. Here's the problem: American stamps can't be used to mail a letter from Canada (not yet, anyway), and just try and find a Canadian stamp in a U.S. convenience store. An IRC solves this dilemma. You buy one at your U.S. post office, slip it into the envelope, and the recipient exchanges it for return postage at his local post office. Simple, huh?

Simple and a potential cash cow. Back in the '20s, Ponzi stopped roaring long enough to notice that IRCs didn't fluctuate with local exchange rates. In other words, the same dollar that bought 20 IRCs in the U.S. could buy over three times that in, say, Italy.

Cha-freakin'-ching!

A creative and ambitious businessman, Ponzi saw an immediate opportunity and seized it. His scheme involved persuading investors to bankroll a massive purchase of IRCs in countries whose economies were still recovering from World War I, and then redeeming them for stamps or cash in America where their value was as much as 500% higher. Promising investors in his Securities Exchange Company 50% interest in 90 days, Ponzi sucked in cash like a Michael Bay blockbuster on a Fourth of July long weekend.

While his IRC scheme was ultimately a bust, Charles Ponzi may take some post-mortem comfort in the fact that the concept spawned a million-and-one multi-level marketing scams ...

There was only one snag. The scheme, though technically legal, was a logistical nightmare. Ponzi couldn't find a cost-effective way to purchase IRCs in sufficient bulk (i.e. to pay a $2,655 bill, he once calculated he needed 53,000 IRCs — the equivalent of seven stacks of paper three feet high) or to transform them into cold, hard cash. So, he did what any self-respecting businessman would do. He made good on his promise to early investors by paying them off with money received from later investors. Within months, the scheme fell apart and Ponzi was up on fraud charges.

While his IRC scheme was ultimately a bust, Charles Ponzi may take some post-mortem comfort in the fact that the concept spawned a million-and-one multi-level marketing scams, most of which flog vitamins worth more than weapons-grade plutonium, and most of which your cousin Albert has enthusiastically boosted at one time or another.

A Layman's Psychoanalysis: Ponzi's cautionary tale is a classic case of a guy whose mind writes checks his body can't cash. He's also a case study in how the best intentions can lead to the worst results.

A Lesson for Laymen: Guys will subvert the truth to obtain an end if they believe that end is ultimately good.

To learn more about Charles Ponzi, take a "peak" at Ponzi's Scheme: The True Story of a Financial Legend *by Mitchell Zuckoff.*

TipBit: Vincent van Gogh'ing, Gogh'ing, Gone

Vincent van Gogh was – how to put it delicately? – a bit of a freak-show during his lifetime. The incident that best captures the Dutch master's, um, quirkiness is the gifting of his ear to a prostitute named Rachel in Arles, France. But it wasn't his whole ear, as the myth perpetuates, only a portion of his left lobe. Like that makes it any less strange.

Here's another piece of van Gogh's life you might not have known: The only painting he sold during his lifetime was *The Red Vineyard* for a mere 400 francs (the rough equivalent of dinner and a movie for two in Troy, Michigan). Compare that bargain-basement deal to the $82.5 million auction price reached for his *Portrait of Dr. Gachet,* sold at Christie's in 1990 to Ryoei Saito (a record for a work of art at the time). That'd be equal to dinner and a movie for about 1.2 million couples in Troy, Michigan.

Stephen Glass: Hotshot Reporter Busted for Fabricating Stories

Monicondoms. The First Church of George Herbert Walker Christ. Pot-smoking young Republicans engaging in orgies (in Washington, D.C., no less). These are but a small sample of the work undertaken by a reporter who took the term "creative non-fiction" far too literally.

Snappy writing notwithstanding, Stephen Glass' feature articles for *The New Republic* and other prominent magazines during the dying years of the millennium came packed with imaginary people, places and events. To buttress his charade, the bookish, twentysomething writer concocted detailed notes, voicemails, faxes, and even went as far as designing fake letterhead, newsletters and a company website.

Glass joined *The New Republic* as an editorial assistant in 1995. Over a three-year period, he also slipped his fib-filled pieces past the fact-checking goalies at *George, Rolling Stone, Harper's*, and other venerable magazines and newspapers. His comeuppance arrived when a reporter from *Forbes Online* followed up on an article Glass had written about a 15-year-old cyberhacker who had extorted tens of thousands of dollars from a company called Jukt Micronics. The jig was up when the facts proved to be pure fiction. I'll spare you the "shattered glass" and "people in glass houses" puns.

A Layman's Psychoanalysis: Another example of blind ambition, Glass' case is instructive in that it demonstrates just how far guys will go in order to advance in their chosen field, and how high they'll pile the b.s. to cover their inadequacies. If Glass had put 10% as much effort into honest reporting, he'd still be a rising star today.

A Lesson for Laymen: Never underestimate the complexity of men's lies — or their impatience to move ahead at work or with the ladies.

For more insights into Glass' psyche, pick up a copy of his novel, The Fabulist, *at your favorite used bookstore or neighborhood garage sale. Or rent* Shattered Glass, *the movie (not my pun). It stars Hayden Christensen, better known as the evil Darth Vader, and he's dreamy!*

TipBit: News for April Fools

The precise origin of April Fools' Day is murky. Many experts believe the tradition arose when our ancestors switched from the Julian to the Gregorian calendar in the 1500s. The dimwitted types who continued to celebrate New Years on April 1st (as per the old calendar) became known as April Fools. Others think the term comes from Mother Nature's frequent attempts to fool us into thinking Spring has arrived. Whatever the origin, April 1st offers a choice opportunity to pull big-time pranks on the people we love. And the media, despite their stodgy image, have jumped into the act with both feet. Here's three of their awesome snow jobs:

1. The Swiss Spaghetti Harvest: Arguably the best media-generated April Fools' dodge is the Swiss Spaghetti Harvest piece that aired on the BBC's *Panorama* on April 1, 1957. Richard Dimbleby's news report explained to viewers that Spring had arrived early in Switzerland, prompting an early spaghetti harvest. In the background video accompanying Dimbleby's voice-over, peasant women were shown harvesting a bumper crop of spaghetti from trees. The pasta's uniform length and bountifulness was credited to years of careful cultivation and the eradication of the dreaded spaghetti weevil.

Calls from over 250 viewers lit up the BBC switchboard after the piece aired, nearly all of them dead-dog serious inquiries about where one could go to view the harvest. It's rumored that *Panorama*'s producer got in on the act, too: he recommended people plant a small tin of spaghetti in tomato sauce to grow their own crop at home.

2. The Taco Liberty Bell: On April 1, 1996, Taco Bell Corp. announced that it had purchased the Liberty Bell from the federal government and was renaming it the Taco Liberty Bell. Apoplectic citizens vowed to tear the National Historic Park in Philadelphia (the keeper of the bell) a new one. A few hours later, however, Taco Bell fessed up to the prank. When asked about the prank later in the day, Mike McCurry (then White House press secretary) stated the Lincoln Memorial had also been sold and would be known forever more as the Ford Lincoln Mercury Memorial.

3. The Burger King Left-Handed Whopper: In 1998, Burger King placed a full-page ad in *USA Today* trumpeting a hot, new menu item: the Left-Handed Whopper. Scientifically designed for millions of southpaw sandwich eaters, the re-tooled Whopper featured the same ingredients as the original, but rotated them 180 degrees in order to redistribute their weight. The weight redistribution, according to the ads, would prevent the toppings from spurting out from the right side of the bun. Thousands of people reportedly asked for the new sandwich. Thousands more requested the right-handed version.

Jayson Blair: Hotshot Reporter Busted for ... Hey, Anyone Else Sense Déjà Vu?

What a difference five years makes. Replace Glass with Blair, *The New Republic* with the *New York Times*, 1998 with 2003 and you get the gist. Oh, and add plagiarism in Blair's case. He scoured the Internet for news stories he could cut and paste into his own to add local color and grace notes. The title of Blair's book? *Burning Down My Masters' House.* The masters' house, by the way, was the *New York Times.* He also burned down the careers of a few senior editors. Enough said.

A Layman's Psychoanalysis: Blair's tale mirrors Glass' so closely, the two are almost interchangeable. The exception is Blair had Glass' downfall as an example of the consequences that might lie ahead. So what was Blair thinking? Simple: He wasn't.

A Lesson for Laymen: Guys don't necessarily learn from the negative consequences of other guy's lies.

Random Aside: At the time this digest was published, Glass' work of fiction was outselling Blair's non-fiction title on amazon.com by a fair margin, proving once and for all you should stick with your strengths.

Ollie Lied, By Golly

Lying does not come easy to me. But we had to weigh in the balance the difference between lives and lies.

— Lieutenant-Colonel Oliver North

Testimony before the joint Congressional hearings into the Iran-Contra affair

TipBit: That's a Cold Shot, Baby

There's an entire myth industry surrounding Walt Disney, which isn't surprising considering he was an intensely private man leading an immensely public entertainment company. Of all the myths surrounding Disney's life, arguably the most thought-provoking is the one that surrounds his death — or the moments immediately prior to his death at least.

Rumor has it that Disney had his body cryogenically frozen just before he died, and now awaits the day when medical technology can re-animate him like a digitally remastered copy of *Cinderella*. Remarkable story, but not even remotely true. Alas, Disney would need a pretty freakin' amazing medical breakthrough to re-animate his ashes, which reside in a crypt in Glendale, California's Forest Lawn Cemetery.

Big Tobacco: Big Fibbers

Cocaine isn't the only big lie. For better than three decades, Big Tobacco's gang of CEOs steadfastly maintained that cigarettes weren't addictive and smoking wasn't harmful to your health. All righty then! Everyone who buys that line stand on your head. Check out these facts from *thetruth.com:*

- ❖ In the 1970s, tobacco companies started making light cigarettes by putting tiny holes in the filters to let extra air mix with the smoke. They found they could get low readings of toxic agents from FTC-type cigarette testing machines.
- ❖ One tobacco company developed a genetically altered tobacco with twice the addictive nicotine of regular tobacco. They code-named it "Y-1."
- ❖ In 1984, one tobacco company referred to new customers as "replacement smokers."
- ❖ An internal tobacco company marketing report from 1989 said, "We believe that most of the strong, positive images for cigarettes and smoking are created by cinema and television."
- ❖ In 1990, a tobacco company put together a plan to stop coroners from listing tobacco as a cause of death on a death certificate.
- ❖ In the mid-'90s, a major tobacco company planned on boosting sales of their cigarettes by targeting a new consumer market: gays and homeless people. They called the plan Project Sub-Culture Urban Marketing. Also known as Project SCUM.
- ❖ The impact of nicotine is jacked up because tobacco companies add ammonia.

A Layman's Psychoanalysis: In the face of mounting evidence to the contrary, the wise men who ran big tobacco for over thirty years would not relent in the view that their product was virtually innocuous. This "the world is flat" groupthink remains ominously prevalent among some of the largest and most powerful organizations in North America today, organizations that substitute doctrine and the party line for actual thinking.

A Lesson for Laymen: Guys, especially in groups, will stick to their guns, even when their guns are loaded with lies, and even when their lies kill people. Guys in groups will also stick together, singing the same tune from the same, suspect song sheet — especially when there's a lot of money at stake.

TipBit: Seven Years to Digest

One of the most resilient wives tales passed from generation to generation is that of chewing gum taking seven years to pass through the digestive tract. Millions of reasonably intelligent gum chewers, if faced with the choice of continuing to gnaw on a putrid stick of stale spearmint or swallowing the sucker, will chose to chew. They can still hear the grating voices of their mothers, admonishing them from years past: "Don't swallow that! It'll take seven years to digest."

Where the seven year figure comes from is anyone's guess, but what's certain is that gum — regardless of its indestructible property in your mouth — doesn't stand a snowball's chance in hell of lasting more than 24 hours in your digestive tract. Not that it'll be digested, mind you.

The wad will simply pass through the system and out the other, um, end without much of a change at all. Kind of like a guy in relationship counseling.

Aldrich Ames: I, Spy

One of the most damaging spies ever to "grace" the halls of CIA headquarters, Aldrich Ames earned $3 million over nine years for the high-level intelligence he provided — to the Russians. In effect, he sold the lives of nearly a dozen U.S. intelligence operatives in the USSR and other countries at bargain basement prices, along with sensitive data worth countless millions.

And he did it all while passing every routine polygraph test administered by the agency. In the end, the fruits of his treason — Rolex watches, designer dresses for his wife, a Jag in the driveway — tipped off investigators. Seems it pays to live within your means when you're selling state secrets. Arrested by the FBI in 1994, Ames is serving life in prison and is hopefully on the receiving end of some good ol' prison lovin'.

A Layman's Psychoanalysis: Ames subverted the interests of every man, woman and child in America for his own, narrow interests. Not only did he place *your* security in jeopardy, Ames' actions directly resulted in the death of many intelligence operatives. All because he coveted nice things (and had been passed over for promotion within the CIA).

A Lesson for Laymen: The shallowness and vindictiveness of man shall not be underestimated.

TipBit: Contempt for the Polygraph from the Man Who Beat It Again and Again

Here's a snippet of a handwritten letter sent by Aldrich Ames to Steven Aftergood at the Federation of American Scientists, showing the former man's contempt for the polygraph. Ames was serving time in the Allenwood federal penitentiary when the letter, postmarked November 28, 2000, was written:

... Like most junk science that just won't die (graphology, astrology and homeopathy come to mind), because of the usefulness or profit their practitioners enjoy, the polygraph stays with us.

Its most obvious use is as a coercive aid to interrogators, lying somewhere on the scale between the rubber truncheon and the diploma on the wall behind the interrogator's desk. It depends upon the overall coerciveness of the setting — you'll be fired, you won't get the job, you'll be prosecuted, you'll go to prison — and the credulous fear the device inspires ...

Bernard Ebbers: From Telecom Cowboy to Telecom Convict

Not many men can claim to have taken a company's market capitalization from multi-multi-billion to sub-sub-zero in the space of a few years. Bernard Ebbers, former CEO of WorldCom, can. And he'll likely have 25 years in prison to contemplate his incredible feat.

The demise of WorldCom comes replete with superlatives. Largest case of fraud in U.S. corporate history. Biggest bankruptcy

in U.S. corporate history. And arguably the highest free-fall from wealth and power in U.S. corporate history.

Not bad for a guy born in Edmonton, Alberta. Ebbers, known at his height of power as the Telecom Cowboy, once worked as a milkman and a bouncer before cutting his business teeth on a chain of motels in Mississippi. He invested in Long Distance Discount Services, Inc. in 1983 and within two years was named its chief executive. By 1995, LDDS had acquired 60 other telecoms and changed its name to WorldCom. Life, she was good.

In 1998, life (briefly) got even better when WorldCom completed its acquisition of MCI Communications for a cool $40 billion price tag. MCI WorldCom's market cap went through the roof.

At his peak in 1999, Ebbers was worth an estimated $1.4 billion and ranked number 174 on the *Forbes 400*. Things started to sour the same year when MCI WorldCom announced its intention to acquire Sprint Communications for a staggering $115 billion. U.S. and European regulators stepped in to squash the buy, just as the entire telecom market started to shrivel (remember all those dot-bombs?), and MCI WorldCom's stock took a dive.

When he stepped down as CEO in 2002, just before the accounting scandal broke, Ebbers' loans were consolidated in a single $408.2 million promissory note to WorldCom. And I bet you thought your Visa bill was high.

Therein lay the problem. Much of the Telecom Cowboy's personal holdings — including Canada's largest working ranch, a minor-league hockey team and a yacht-building company — had been purchased with loans backed by Ebbers' personal WorldCom stock. When margin calls flooded in, WorldCom's Board of Directors authorized huge loans and guarantees to the CEO so he wouldn't have to sell off his shares. (It doesn't look very good to investors when CEOs dump their own stock.) To make matters worse, Ebbers pressured WorldCom's Chief Financial Officer, Scott Sullivan, to cook the books, making WorldCom appear far more profitable than it was and protecting the stock from even bigger losses. That's a colossal no-no, folks.

When he stepped down as CEO in 2002, just before the accounting scandal broke, Ebbers' loans were consolidated in a single $408.2 million promissory note to WorldCom. And I bet you thought your Visa bill was high.

In July 2002, with the full weight of the scandal bearing down, WorldCom filed for bankruptcy to shield its mammoth $41 billion debt from creditors. Yes, you read that right: $41 *billion*. To put this figure into perspective, consider the highest-ranking Gross National Product (the total value of final goods and services produced in one year by a country's nationals) of all the countries in the world in 2003. WorldCom's debt, translated into GNP, would have been good for the 55th highest spot out of 216 countries (just edging out Libya's GNP of $40.5 billion).

A Layman's Psychoanalysis: Ebbers arguably had it all — and tried everything in his power to keep it all: Subterfuge; misdirection; and the blame game. Playing dumb and pointing his finger at Scott Sullivan was Ebbers' last-gasp attempt to avoid the liar label. Nice try, pal.

A Lesson for Laymen: Guys will do anything to keep their name out of the mud (except, of course, foregoing the deceptive activity that drags it into the mud in the first place). Guys will also try to pin the blame on others: CFOs; close friends; public-school teachers; porn-site webmasters; society at large. Anything and anyone to avoid culpability.

TipBit: If You Don't Know Abramoff, You Don't Know Jack

Sorry, I lied about not touching on prevaricating politicians in this chapter. But this story's just too juicy to pass up — and it has the potential to reach into the highest office in the land.

Earlier this year, Republican lobbyist Jack Abramoff — dubbed "The Man Who Bought Washington" by *Time* magazine — pleaded guilty to three felony counts of conspiracy, fraud and tax evasion. *Yawn.* Another crooked lobbyist, you say. So what? The real legs on this story, dear reader, is the plea bargain Abramoff made with federal prosecutors, who secured his full cooperation in their investigation of congressional corruption by tossing out the maximum 30-year prison sentence. Jack is said to be cooperating fully. And rumor has it many heavy hitters will be whacked by his testimony. Oh, did I mention Jack raised at least $100,000 for the President's re-election campaign?

The pitch-perfect chorus of denials of any and all connections to Abramoff coming from Capitol Hill's political elite (and the Office of the President) in the aftermath of the plea deal makes the Vienna Boys' Choir sound like a tone-deaf barbershop quartet. Who's lying? We'll have to stay tuned.

Fred Gilliland: A Love for Two-for-One Coupons Knows No Boundaries

How's this for an example of a greedy knob? Fred Gilliland, a pathological Canadian con artist who scammed nearly $30 million from 200 investors in the U.S., Canada and the United Kingdom, met his downfall thanks to an insatiable appetite for two-for-one dining coupons.

Gilliland ran "high return, risk free" investment scams. Wanted in Florida for fraud, conspiracy and racketeering, he fled to Vancouver, British Columbia in 2000, set himself up in a $1.7 million house, and then bought a cherry ride: a BMW 745i. Indicted *in absentia* by a Florida grand jury in October 2001, Gilliland was named a fugitive by the FBI and the following year had civil action filed against him by the Securities and Exchange Commission (SEC) for securities fraud. (The SEC obtained a $10 million default judgment.) In July 2003, Canada's intrepid Royal Canadian Mounted Police swooped in, busting the crook at his upscale Vancouver digs. A court-appointed SEC receiver sold the house and pocketed the proceeds, but the con artist wasn't out of commission yet.

Three of Gilliland's supporters (no doubt terrific judges of character) put up $750,000 bail to put the man back on the street. Gilliland surrendered his passport and agreed not to leave Canada pending extradition proceedings. Less than half a year later, however, he was operating under the name Fred Lane and

Zzzzzz
CYA:
ottawa

living in Yaletown, a trendy urban community located on the False Creek side of downtown Vancouver. And as you may have guessed, the new Fred was soon up to old Fred's tricks.

TipBit: CBC Announces A Fresh New Series for the Fall Lineup

Watch for a gritty and slightly more liberal new drama this fall, brought to you by the Canadian Broadcasting Corporation. *CYA: Ottawa* follows the exploits of a tight-knit gang of Sussex Drive insiders as they disavow any knowledge of illicit sponsorship money and secret loans to golf courses. Features ten times less flag waving than *CYA: Washington* — and ten times less excitement.

But Gilliland/Lane picked the wrong mark when he chose "Brian," a Vancouver private investigator, for his next investment pitch: sketchy penny stocks. Gilliland/Lane talked Brian into investing $300 Gs, whose value flew south faster than Canadian retirees in November. By early 2005, two-thirds of Brian's investment had evaporated and Gilliland/Lane couldn't provide a good explanation why. Brian, the PI, did what PIs do best. He started digging.

Despite the Florida indictment against him, Gilliland jumped on the cross-border dining offer like a fat kid on a Smartie. Make that a *stupid* fat kid on a Smartie.

He didn't like what he unearthed. He discovered Gilliland/ Lane's true identity, as well as his fugitive status in the U.S. So Brian decided to take Gilliland down using the oldest trick in the book. He made his arch enemy his "best friend."

As Gilliland's best bud, Brian learned about the con man's taste for two-for-one dining. One day, he casually mentioned he had two-for-one coupons for a great eatery called Brewster's in Point Roberts, Washington — a tiny nub of American soil orphaned by the 49th parallel. Despite the Florida indictment against him, Gilliland jumped on the cross-border dining offer like a fat kid on a Smartie. Make that a *stupid* fat kid on a Smartie.

The two men rolled across the sleepy border crossing at Point Roberts in Brian's 4x4 on March 12, 2005. Within minutes, the car was surrounded by U.S. undercover agents (tipped by Brian) and a bewildered Gilliland was in handcuffs.

Just goes to show you: there ain't no free lunch.

A Layman's Psychoanalysis: Gilliland is a classic predator, preying on trusting people to obtain his nefarious ends. He's also a prime example of that extremely dangerous type of liar whose mind spins an intricate spider web of lies, but ultimately traps the wrong body with its stickiness.

A Lesson for Laymen: Once a guy's a liar, he's always a liar. And if a guy's a moron ... well, he's just a moron.

TipBit: A Million Little Lies

Here's one piece of advice for those of you thinking of committing your life story to paper in the hopes of attracting a top-rank publisher, a fat advance against royalties and multiple appearances on the daytime-television circuit. If your life is as exciting as a ten-pound bag of potting soil, for heaven's sake, DO NOT EMBELLISH! Not unless you wish to suffer the fate of memoirist James Frey, author of *A Million Little Pieces.*

Dubbed "The Book that Kept Oprah Awake at Night," *AMLP's* graphic tale of addiction and redemption was heavy on bodily fluids and light on facts. Burned in the media glare ignited by *thesmokinggun.com's* accidental outing, Frey defended his embellishments before the court of public opinion as artistic license — a license that permitted the use of "emotional" truth in place of "actual" truth in order to bring the book's underlying message of hope into more poignant (and profitable) relief. Memoirs, in case you missed the hullabaloo early in 2006, are supposed to be grounded in "actual" truth. That's why they're found in the non-fiction section of bookstores.

Still, the guy sold a gazillion copies and made a gazillion bucks thanks to Oprah's endorsement and the hullabaloo. So, forget my advice and embellish away. Long live "truthiness" and Oprah's Book Club!

There are three kinds of lies:
lies, damn lies, and statistics.
— Benjamin Disraeli
British Prime Minister (1804 – 1881)

A deception that elevates us
is dearer than a host of low truths.
— Marina Tsvetaeva
Russian poet (1892–1941)

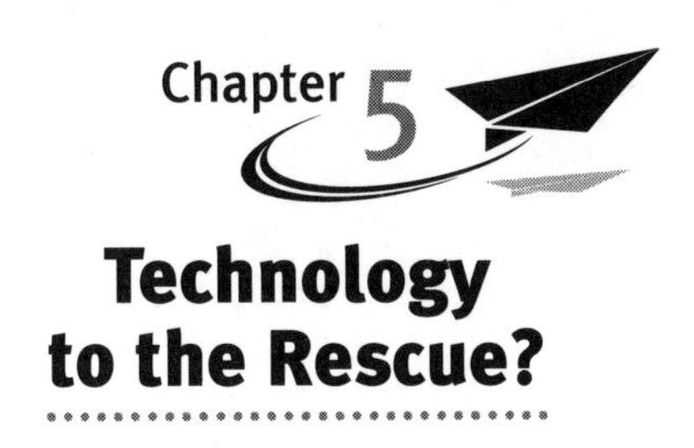

Technology to the Rescue?

Sin has many tools, but a lie is the handle that fits them all.
—Oliver Wendell Holmes, Jr.
Noted American jurist (1841-1935)

Besides being strange, people make mistakes. We want to believe what we are told, regardless of the source. We're forced to rely on senses that can't always be trusted. Busting bald-faced liars — especially the ones closest to us — is one aspect of our being where fallibility and sensory limitation put us at a disadvantage.

Thanks to our infinite capacity for invention, however, we keep developing innovative ways to take our imperfections out of the loop. And these aren't just recent developments. The age-old problem of mendacity has seen age-old attempts by societies to develop systematic processes for busting b.s.'ers. In typical old-school style, many of the processes were a tad harsh. Here's a quick sample:

- Ancient Hindus forced suspects to chew rice and spit it out on a leaf from a sacred tree. If the rice came out dry, the suspect was considered guilty. Nasty stuff followed.

❖ Arabia's Bedouin tribes, nomads of the desert, made suspected fibbers lick a hot iron. If the tongue burned, then the suspect was lying. Hey, is it just me or did anyone else get an image of Ken Starr, Black & Decker Press'N'Go in hand, looming menacingly over Bill Clinton?

❖ Trials by ordeal were a crowd favorite among ancient cultures. Like the Bedouin version of the "red-hot fork in the pie" trick, most involved the judicious application of heat. One trial had the suspect walk barefoot across scorching-hot iron. If the burns healed after three days, the poor bastard was declared innocent (and this before the days of Bactine disinfectant spray). Another version made the suspect submerge his arm in a cauldron of boiling water. No blisters? No lie.

And no picnic for the accused. We've modernized our techniques for catching liars over the centuries, casting off our fixation on inflicting pain like the guy who spent his childhood grilling ants under a magnifying glass, but now sticks to torturing his co-workers with banal conversation. Same effect; less smoke.

Follow me now as I take you through the major technological innovations that have brought us that much closer to consistently busting bald-faced liars. And, please, leave your magnifying glasses behind.

We've modernized our techniques for catching liars over the centuries, casting off our fixation on inflicting pain like the guy who spent his childhood grilling ants under a magnifying glass, but now sticks to torturing his co-workers with banal conversation. Same effect; less smoke.

TipBit: Toss another Witch on the Barbie

In 1692, Salem, Massachusetts wasn't the smartest place on earth to set up housekeeping for people with quirky personalities or malformed noses. Back then, it didn't take much to get labeled a witch, and everyone knows that Salem's Puritans spent more time burning witches at the stake than shopping for Easter bonnets at Wal-Mart, right?

There are two things wrong with this assumption. Firstly, Wal-Mart hadn't yet spread its retail tentacles around the planet and, secondly, no witches were burned at the stake during Witchstock 1692. Of the 150 unlucky souls accused of witchcraft, 20 were sentenced to death.

Of the 20, 19 were hanged and one was stoned. Yeah, the bad kind of stoned.

The Polygraph

The first "polygraph" containing the essential features used in the modern device was developed by heart specialist Sir James Mackenzie in 1906. It was used strictly for medical purposes, though. But as early as 1908, Harvard professor Hugo Munsterberg, an innovator in the psycho-physiological study of emotion, proposed measuring the three physical properties now commonly used in lie detection: pulse rate, breathing and skin conductivity.

In 1915, a student of Munsterberg's named William Marston began a series of experiments using blood pressure in the detection of deception. He also recorded breathing patterns and experimented with skin-resistance measurements. Dr. Marston publicized his lie detector extensively and tried to get Bruno Hauptmann, alleged kidnapper of the Lindbergh baby, to take the test.

TipBit: Oh, the Magic Lasso and Do-Me Boots Make Sense Now

Writing under the pseudonym Charles Moulton, William Marston also created Wonder Woman, the DC Comics character renowned for her Lasso of Truth and other, um, assets. In the first of several popular psychology books, *Emotions of Normal People* (published in 1928), Dr. Marston discussed emotional states in terms of "elementary behavior units" in the activities of dominance, compliance, submission and inducement. Among his many theories was one that argued America would become a matriarchic state in which women would use sexual enslavement to achieve dominance over men. Millions of comic book fans are still awaiting its arrival. Millions of married men know it's already here.

It was John Larston, however, who finally put together a true "polygraph" — an instrument that simultaneously recorded blood pressure, pulse and respiration continuously throughout a test session. His device was used extensively in criminal investigations and met with great success and acclaim — until it was appropriated by Midas for its lame television commercials.

TipBit: Everything Old is New Again

The principles on which polygraph detection depend are more old-school than you might imagine. The first record of systematic methods for the psycho-physiological detection of concealed information is found in the *Veda*, the earliest record of human experience. Thought to be well over 10,000 years old, the *Veda* was passed down orally for generations by pundits with too much time on their hands. (This was before the days of "Must-See TV.") Ancient Vedic HMOs used a person's pulse to diagnose a variety of physical, mental, emotional and spiritual imbalances — including guilt over past misdeeds and misrepresentations — and then screwed the patient over with limited, overpriced treatment options.

The operating principle behind the modern polygraph machine is simple. The device measures a subject's pulse rate, respiration and skin conductivity, simultaneously and continuously recording the values on a graph (hence, the name *poly*graph). The polygraph operator (typically a specially trained forensic psychophysiologist) establishes a baseline recording by posing questions whose correct answers are already known. Essentially, the operator calibrates the device to the subject's unique physiological "fingerprint." Any deviation from the established baseline for truthful answers can then be interpreted as a sign of deception.

In the most extreme cases, a completely innocent but Nervous Nelly could come across looking like a liar. Heck, even a bout of constipation could pin a bum rap on you.

But the very principles that make the polygraph effective can potentially make it problematic. Many factors can affect a person's pulse rate, respiration and skin conductivity. In the most extreme cases, a completely innocent but Nervous Nelly could come across looking like a liar. Heck, even a bout of constipation could pin a bum rap on you. Even worse, a stone-cold psycho can beat the machine. So too can an ordinary guy who's convinced his lies are truth. For this reason, polygraph results are not admissible evidence in many courtrooms.

Does this mean the device is useless? Far from it. Jack Trimarco, an expert polygraph examiner and consultant whose case history includes the Oklahoma City bombing, the Unabomber investigation and the 1993 World Trade Center bombing, cites that experienced forensic psycho-physiologists can filter out the effects of nervousness and achieve remarkably accurate results. Liars take note!

TipBit: Stupid Suspect + Fake Lie Detector = One Confession

Out of small-town Pennsylvania comes a legend so bizarre, so disturbing, so heinous that its mere mention will send you screaming into the night ... or rolling your eyes; one of the two.

Either the Radnor Police Department or the Bucks County Police Department (does it really matter?) busted a felon in the early '60s by hooking him up to a lie detector. The catch is they cobbled the device together using a metal colander from the station's kitchen, some old shoelaces and a Xerox photocopier.

The cops knew their suspect was guilty, but they needed a confession. Rather than use the time-honored method of beating one out of him, they instead set a colander on the guy's head and connected it to the photocopier with a pair of shoelaces. Unbeknownst to the guilty party, the cops also inserted a piece of paper into the machine, neatly embossed with the phrase "It's a lie." An officer then obligingly pressed the copy button in response to every response the guy offered. The suspect, whose I.Q. rivaled that of an untreated fence post, ultimately came clean.

While the source of the tale is hard to pin down, urban-legend experts agree the story is rooted in fact. The ploy was even featured in a *Dragnet* episode during its 1967 – 70 renaissances, with Sergeant Joe Friday doing the interrogation and Officer Gannon working the photocopier.

The Truth about Truth Serums

The rationale behind truth serums is the same one that gives us the old saying, *in vino veritas:* There is truth in wine.

Barbiturates such as scopolamine, sodium amytal and sodium pentothal were trumpeted in the early 20th century as a means for unlocking the truth from the lying masses. Like alcohol, they work to lower inhibitions, making the subject loose and "chatty." But lowering inhibitions doesn't necessarily lead to honesty. (Judging by the uninhibited conversations I've overheard in dozens of bars in dozens of countries, quite the opposite could be said.)

So, a person to whom a truth serum is administered can still talk through the back of his neck with the best of 'em. As an added bonus, he'll probably brag incessantly about how much money he made on tech stocks in the '90s.

A Lie by Any Other Name

Talk Through the Back of Your Neck *(v.)* To make unbelievable claims. The opposite of a straight-ahead statement, which would come out of your mouth.

TipBit: The One Thing a Good Cup of Joe Can't Cure

Thinking about drinking? More accurately, are you thinking about sobering up for the girlfriend after a night of heavy drinking? Your buddies would have you believe that quaffing a tall mild or ten at the local Starbucks will bring you back to earth after a blender bender. But the odds of sobering up on coffee are as likely as finding a maple-glazed donut in a Starbucks' pastry case. The caffeine'll just make you a jittery bag of hammers.

Beware of Software

Whereas polygraphs rely on measuring your pulse rate, respiration and skin conductivity, and truth serums rely on sinking your inhibitions to the same level reached at last year's homecoming bash (now referred to as "A Beer Funnel Too Far"), recently developed software relies on your voice to reveal your lying ways.

The software works by analyzing voice fluctuations usually inaudible to the human ear. Stress and anxiety can cause muscle tension and reduce blood flow to the vocal cords, which in turn produces a distinctive pattern of sound waves. The software deciphers the pattern and determines, without feeling or remorse, whether you sneaked a fib into the conversation.

TipBit: Voice Analyzing Software in Action

Time magazine tested one software maker's program during the October 2000 presidential election debate between then Texas Governor George W. Bush and incumbent Vice President Al Gore. The test results showed Bush was a lot less certain and more likely to exaggerate than Gore.

According to the companies flogging the programs, accuracy of detection ranges from 85% to an astounding 99%. As an added bonus, the voice doesn't have to be "live"; a conversation over a phone line or a recording can be analyzed just as accurately as a face-to-face encounter.

But buyers beware: Some high-profile mendacity experts question whether these claims are founded in good science or great marketing. Jack Trimarco recently conducted a feasibility study for a major government department and, after rigorous testing, found the accuracy of the software was no better than a flip of a coin.

Nevertheless, the software has already found a home in organizations specializing in anti-terrorism, counter-narcotics, covert-counter intelligence, arson investigation and insurance fraud. The private sector is also jumping on board and using it for — *gulp!* — employment screening and examinations.

Perhaps the days of the padded résumé are numbered?

fMRI: Quick, Call the Thought Police

If you have the time and the financial resources, take your suspected liar to the nearest hospital and book an MRI. Studies of functional Magnetic Resonance Imaging (fMRI) testing — the kind normally used to detect brain tumors — have found that telling a lie and telling the truth require different brain activities.

It's true! By monitoring changes in the flow of oxygenated blood to the brain, fMRI testing goes right to the "heart" of the matter — the very place where lies are spawned. And, more importantly, a place beyond the suspect's conscious control.

In one study, researchers gave volunteer test subjects an envelope containing a playing card and told them to hide it in their pocket and not divulge its identity. The volunteers were then placed in an MRI scanner and grilled (hmm, maybe that's not the best way to describe it) as to the face value of their dirty little secret. To make a long story short, the scans found that lying and honesty produce different brain activities. Here's how the study leader, the intrepid Dr. Daniel Langleben, described the results:

"Sections of the brain that exercise a significant role in how humans pay attention and monitor and control errors were, on average, more active in volunteers when they were lying than when they were telling the truth."

> S&M inferences aside, the findings by Dr. Langleben and other research teams will likely lead to better methods of lie detection in the future.

These sections of the brain include the *anterior cingulate gyrus* and parts of the prefrontal and premotor cortex. If you think of "the truth" as the response your brain automatically wants to give, then telling a lie requires increased activity in those regions of your brain involved in inhibition and control.

Inhibition and control. Sounds kinky, doesn't it? S&M inferences aside, the findings by Dr. Langleben and other research teams will likely lead to better methods of lie detection in the future.

Torture: The Court of Last Resort

Compelling intransigent fabricators to fess up sometimes calls for harsh measures. While not "technological" in the strictest sense of the word, methods of torture do involve the use of resources beyond our own senses to unveil the truth. And before representatives from Amnesty International arrive to kick down my door, the techniques below are provided in jest. Lighten up, already.

In the Convention Against Torture of 1984, torture is defined as "any act by which severe pain or suffering, whether physical or mental, is intentionally inflicted on a person for such purposes as obtaining from him or a third person information or a confession, punishing him for an act he or a third person has committed or is suspected of having committed, or intimidating or coercing him or a third person for any reason based on discrimination of any kind, when such pain or suffering is inflicted by or at the instigation of or with the consent or acquiescence of a public official or other person acting in an official capacity."

Got all that? Kudos if you do. I needed a divining rod and a flashlight to find the point. (Note to the United Nations: Take the above sentence to a good New York tailor. I'm sure she could have it shortened by the end of the week.) It's important to know what we're dealing with, though, so I'll break it down for you: *Pain, suffering, intimidation* and *coercion*. For the married couples reading this, you're already 90% there. Now, let's go all the way.

❖ **Stress Positions:** Often times, the simplest methods of torture are the most effective. Stress positions involve placing the subject in the most uncomfortable position your deviant imagination can summon. The longer the duration, the better. **Suggested Technique:** Hand your husband a pamphlet for ballroom-dance lessons offered at the local Y. Make him sign up for 10 weeks worth and use the added threat of 10 weeks of Salsa lessons as the clincher to get the truth.

❖ **Behavioral Coercion:** Essentially, this method involves forcing the subject to do something he wouldn't ordinarily do in a million years. **Suggested Technique:** Rent Season One *and* Season Two of *Sex and the City* and tell him, without a hint of irony, that he'll be rubbing your feet from the opening credits 'til the final Special Features segment unless he comes clean.

❖ **Sensory Deprivation:** A popular method with college lecturers, sensory deprivation, well, deprives sensory input from the subject and reduces life to a barren shell. **Suggested Technique:** Confiscate the TV remote and ban all reading material from the bathroom. That'll get him singing in no time.

❖ **Noise Pollution:** This nasty method involves bombarding the subject with distressing levels of acoustic energy for prolonged periods or, preferably, at random intervals. **Suggested Technique:** Place subject in the living room and render immobile by whatever means is most convenient. Screaming, "You sit there and you listen to this!" should work fine. Place three Christina Aguilera CDs, two Vanilla Ice CDs and one William Shatner CD in the six-pack player. Set to random shuffle and rush out the door for your weekend spa retreat before the first note hits the speakers. Be sure to remove all pets from the home before attempting.

❖ **Electroshock Therapy:** This method is pretty much self-explanatory without going into the gory details and rendering this digest unsellable. **Suggested Technique:** Get a car battery, some jumper cables and vow to wire his gonads for sound unless he spills the beans. Trust me, the visual alone with have him squealing like a coulrophobic at a circus.

Oh what a tangled web we weave,
When first we practise to deceive!
— Sir Walter Scott, *Marmion,* Canto vi. Stanza 17
Scottish author & novelist (1771 – 1832)

Even More Brilliant Ways to Bust Any Bald-Faced Liar

A lie told often enough becomes the truth.
—Vladimir Lenin
Russian Communist politician & revolutionary (1870–1924)

Just when you thought you were out, more brilliant tips pull you back in.

In Chapter One we discussed the weird and wonderful ways men and women lie. In Chapters Two and Three, you learned dozens of ways to spot the signposts of deception. Chapter Four let you see the handiwork of some of the most notorious male liars (and you realized, in comparison, that your partner's fibs really aren't that bad). And in the last chapter, you glimpsed a world of technological potential for busting bald-faced liars. In other words, you are now armed to the gills to get to the truth.

But maybe you feel you need a bit more help. Maybe you're up against a particularly skillful liar — someone with a tongue of silver, the eyes of a poker champ and the face of an angel, with the imagination of Stephen King and a photographic memory for details.

That sucks. Don't fret, though. The additional techniques provided in this chapter will help you penetrate any fish story and reel in the truth. Let's sharpen that hook!

A Lie by Any Other Name

Fish Story ***(n.)*** A tall tale or exaggeration, especially of one's own exploits. Derived from the propensity of fishermen to stretch the size of their catch — and their bait and tackle.

Hire a Wringer to Bust a Liar

One way to bust a bald-faced liar is to hire a wringer ... someone who's specially trained to wring the truth out of a suspect. Several professions deal with liars all the time; cops, judges, psychologists and CIA agents are ones that spring immediately to mind. A study published in the journal *Psychological Science* a while back tested the ability of these professionals to sift truth from fiction. Here's what was found:

❖ Cops nabbed liars 50% of the time. That's about the same as an untrained group of people. Next time you get pinched for speeding, plead innocence. Odds are even-steven the cop'll believe you.

❖ Judges faired a bit better than the cops and the average Joe. Their success rate in judging the truth? 62%.

❖ Psychologists did even better, averaging correct diagnoses of mendacity up to 68% of the time.

❖ For spotting liars, however, nothing beats a CIA agent. These men and women, who receive "special training" in

reading expressions and gestures, busted bald-faced liars 73% of the time. Makes you wonder whether some "special props" were employed to help boost their average. Hey, anyone seen my car battery and jumper cables?

TipBit: The National Liars' Hall of Fame

No kidding. It's located in Dannebrog, Nebraska, a town whose population mirrors that of a well-attended Toastmasters meeting. It was the brainchild of humorist Roger Welsh, author and former commentator on CBS's *Sunday Morning.*

Curios on display in the Hall of Fame include multicolored golf balls kept in a box labeled "Golf balls as big as hail" and a fly swatter with a hole in its mesh, accompanied by certificate of approval from the Society for the Prevention of Cruelty to Flies.

Incredibly, upward of 700 people visit the Liars' Hall of Fame every year from all 50 states and 28 foreign countries. My question is this: Did those foreign visitors travel all the way to Nebraska for golf balls and goofy fly swatters?

Control the Environment and Bust the Liar

The following tips will let you, the reader, function as a kick-arse interrogator. Try it on the kids today! Remember: All are innocent until you decide they aren't.

- ❖ Place the alleged liar in a quiet, preferably private setting. One free of distractions and interruptions works best. Try to minimize any extraneous "noise" that might drown out the subject's baseline behavior and distract your focus. You also want to avoid any potential witnesses in case you have to crank it up a notch.

- ❖ Start by asking puff-ball questions that have nothing to do with the real subject. Throw a few thought-provoking sliders out for consideration to see how the subject handles them, but make them benign as well. The point of this stage of the interrogation is to relax the subject, lull him into a false sense of security, and to establish the all-important baseline that'll trip him up when it comes time to get to the truth.

- ❖ Observe and record the answers to the questions. Make sure to note the grammar the subject uses, his body lan-

ABANDON HOPE, ALL YE WHO ENTER HERE.

Think Vincenzo Coccotti in *True Romance*. He gives Dennis Hopper's character a terminal case of the third degree. This is the standard you should strive for.

guage, tone of voice and so on. You'll need this information shortly.

- Now it's time to get into the meat of the interrogation. Start asking the real questions, going beyond the point of what you want to know. Then, just when the subject thinks it's over, re-ask some of the questions and look for discrepancies. These are the "tells" — the subtle and not-so-subtle verbal and non-verbal giveaways that will bust a bald-faced liar. If you spot any, go for the jugular.

Think Vincenzo Coccotti in *True Romance.* He gives Dennis Hopper's character a terminal case of the third degree. This is the standard you should strive for. As much as his "I'm the anti-Christ" speech, Coccotti's "pantomime" speech and ruthless interrogation techniques cement him as a classic film villain and a fan favorite.

Become a Better Liar Yourself

In *Manhunter,* William Peterson (Gil Grissom on *CSI: Crime Scene Investigation*) plays a detective who has to climb inside the mind of a psychopath to catch a serial killer. Awesome movie — and an awesome way to bust a bald-faced liar. To snag a fibber, think like a fibber. Here are five final tips on how you can get away with lying:

- Avoid contact with the people you're tossing fibs at. Years of research have proven one thing: if you don't know a guy's "baseline" behavior, it's next to impossible to know whether he's lying. A guy's baseline behavior is simply the way he normally acts, talks, smells, etc. when he isn't lying. If you can avoid prior contact with your mark, your inability to look them in the eye or speak without tripping over your tongue might be attributed to years of drug use or a liberal-arts education, instead of your dastardly desire to sell them 40 acres of swamp land outside Tampa.

- Don't give a toss about the people you're tossing fibs at. It's easier to lie to someone you don't give a fig about. If you try to lie to your significant other, the psychological pressure associated with getting caught ratchets up and your baseline behavior gets all messed up.

❖ If you *do* give a toss about the people you're tossing fibs at, practice first. Practice may not make you a perfect liar, but it will certainly make you a better one. Rehearsing lets you — as psychologists like to say — distance yourself from the lie. The greater the distance, the better your chances of convincing your fiancée that nothing happened at the stag party last night.

❖ The devil is in the details. So's the effectiveness of a lie. Like the best novels, the best lies are chock full of specifics: specific times, specific activities, specific accomplices. The best specifics are those that can't be verified, but make sure you cover your butt on those that can be verified (i.e. if you use your friends as part of your charade, make sure they are down with the details). And, finally, be sure to remember the web of details you weave – or they'll come back to bite your backside.

❖ The last and possibly best tip for passing off your lies as truth is to believe them. Convince yourself that you're spouting the gospel when you're really shoveling manure from a sitting position and it'll be much easier to convince a Doubting Thomas that you're Saint Thomas. *Seinfeld's* George Costanza had it right: "It's not a lie if you believe it." It's probably borderline sociopathic, though.

If you can avoid prior contact with your mark, your inability to look them in the eye or speak without tripping over your tongue might be attributed to years of drug use or a liberal-arts education, instead of your dastardly desire to sell them 40 acres of swamp land outside Tampa.

Repetition does not transform a lie into a truth.
— Franklin D. Roosevelt, radio address, October 26, 1939
32nd president of U.S. (1882 – 1945)

The Last Word

Hey, you made it to the end. Congratulations! So many people never get all the way through the books they purchase — even when the books are designed to be brisk like this digest. Go out and reward yourself.

If you're standing in the bookstore and have just flipped to this page from the Table of Contents, however, no reward for you! You've flipped past a lot of great tips and a ton of great laughs. Don't believe me? Read on.

If you skipped here from the Table of Contents, you missed out on the chance to understand why men and women spin the yarns they do in Chapter One. You missed the whole self-oriented/other-oriented spiel, as well as the part about which people are the most — and least — likely to lie. Oh, and don't forget that disturbing survey regarding women's deception toward their partners. Armed with this chapter's expert knowledge, you would have been more forgiving of the next tall tale tossed your way. Or, if you'd read the survey, more suspicious of your wife on her next girls' night out.

If you just arrived here without visiting Chapter Two and Chapter Three, you didn't catch the freshest and funniest tips for spotting the verbal and non-verbal signs of deceit. We're talking dozens of the best tips, here. Without these insights, how will you know if your boyfriend's stammering and erratic body language are signs of deception or signs of anaphylactic shock?

If you flipped here without stopping at Chapter Four, you forsook (there's a word you don't see often) the mind-blowing lies of some mind-boggling liars, as well as some shrewd psychoanalysis of the lying male's mind by an utterly unqualified psychoanalyst.

If you bypassed Chapter Five, you passed by the opportunity to learn which technological tools are bringing people closer to the truth, and which are just plain bunk. You also bypassed some handy torture techniques that may be illegal in some states and provinces.

Finally, if you blew off Chapter Six, you also blew the chance to scoop up even more brilliant tips on busting bald-faced liars. And in this day and age, you need all the help you can get.

So, if you're a reader who made it through all of the above, go out and celebrate. If you're a reader who skipped here from another part of the digest, go back now and read it from cover to cover. And if you're a reader who's still standing in a bookstore mulling over the purchase, go to the checkout counter and buy it. Trust me: the rewards you'll receive are more than worth the list price.

Honest.

Cool Resources

20 Books

If this digest whetted your appetite for more research on the subject of lying, you could do much worse than checking out the 20 fine books listed alphabetically below. Each takes its own unique approach to lies, liars and the art/science of lying. And each will aid you in your quest to become a lie-detecting ninja!

A Treasury of Deception: Liars, Misleaders, Hoodwinkers, and the Extraordinary True Stories of History's Greatest Hoaxes, Fakes and Frauds by Michael Farquhar, May 2005.

Book of Lies by Essential Works, Malcom Green and Thomas Eaton, October 2005. (Companion volume to *Book of Secrets.*)

The Book of Lies: Schemes, Scams, Fakes, and Frauds That Have Changed the Course of History and Affect Our Daily Lives by M. Hirsh Goldberg, March 1990. (Not to be confused with occult-master Aleister Crowley's *The Book of Lies.*)

Cheaters: 180 Telltale Signs Mates Are Cheating and How to Catch Them by Raymond B. Green with Marcella Bakur Weiner, October 2002.

Deception Detection: Winning The Polygraph Game by Charles Clifton, May 1991.

Detecting Malingering and Deception: Forensic Distortion Analysis, Second Edition by Harold V. Hall and Joseph G. Poirier, November 2000. (Caution: Heavy lifting required.)

Frauds, Deceptions, and Swindles by Carl Sifakis, April 2001.

Is He Cheating on You?: 829 Telltale Signs by Ruth Houston, September 2002.

The Liar's Tale: A History of Falsehood by Jeremy Campbell, November 2002.

Lies! Lies!! Lies!!!: The Psychology of Deceit by Charles V. Ford, M.D., January 1996.

Never Be Lied To Again: How to Get the Truth In 5 Minutes Or Less In Any Conversation Or Situation by David J. Lieberman (Ph.D.), May 1998.

On Bullshit by Harry G. Frankfurt, January 2005.

The Post-Truth Era: Dishonesty and Deception in Contemporary Life by Ralph Keyes, October 2004.

Telling Lies: Clues to Deceit in the Marketplace, Politics, and Marriage (Revised and Updated Edition) by Paul Ekman, September 2001.

The Truth About Lying: How to Spot a Lie and Protect Yourself from Deception by Stan B. Walters, November 2000.

The Truth (with jokes) by Al Franken, October 2005.

The Varnished Truth: Truth Telling and Deceiving in Ordinary Life by David Nyberg, January 1995.

When Presidents Lie: A History of Official Deception and Its Consequences by Eric Alterman, September 2004.

Why We Lie: The Evolutionary Roots of Deception and the Unconscious Mind by David Livingston Smith, July 2004.

Your Call Is Important to Us: The Truth About Bullshit by Laura Penny, July 2005.

10 Movies

If a picture is worth a thousand words, then a movie must be worth a million. And if slogging through more pages of text isn't your idea of a great time, try renting these 10 titles from your favorite video store.

The Adventures of Baron Munchausen (1989). You can score this classic at any decent video store. Where to score the tab of acid that should accompany its viewing is your problem.

Billy Liar (1963). One of John Schlesinger's earliest films. It follows Billy, a young chap with a fairly dreary life, who spends most of his time daydreaming about a land where he's a hero. When his fictions leak out of his head through his mouth, however, things turn topsy-turvy and Billy's credibility takes a nosedive.

The Falcon and the Snowman (1985). Another Schlesinger film (coincidentally). Based on a true story, Timothy Hutton plays Christopher Boyce, an all-American lad turned peddler of state secrets to the USSR. Also features Sean Penn as Boyce's best friend and inept accomplice. A fascinating tale of two former alter boys who descend into a well of deception — and crack under the pressure.

The Great Gatsby (1974). Odds are you studied F. Scott Fitzgerald's novel in high school English. The third film adaptation stars Robert Redford as Jay Gatsby, whose mysterious persona fuels Nick Carraway's imagination. Nick tells the story, and he's not the most reliable narrator.

Jakob the Liar (1999). Discover the power of positive prevarications! Robin Williams plays a Jewish shopkeeper whose fictitious news broadcasts buoy the spirit of fellow residents in Warsaw's miserable ghetto as the end of World War II approaches.

Liar Liar (1997). Hey, I already told you to go rent this.

Sex, Lies and Videotape (1989). James Spader has a penchant for — you guessed it — sex, lies and videotape. Features more erotic triangles than Euclidian geometry. Also stars Peter Gallagher, before he grew out his eyebrows and started hanging out in Orange County, CA.

Telling Lies in America (1997). Check out who else's career Kevin Bacon has touched in this story of a boy from Hungary who feels he has to fib to fit into 1960s America. The wicked pompadour on Bacon's character almost makes it worth the price of the rental. The lack of random, full-frontal nudity on Bacon's character definitely makes it worth the price.

True Lies (1994). Long before he started spinning for the people of California, Governor Schwarzenegger led Jamie Lee Curtis down the garden path as a spy-masquerading-as-saleman-while-saving-America-from-terrorists. How many guys today can relate to that? Look for a brilliant performance by Bill Paxton as a less impressive, but far more realistic car-salesman-masquerading-as-spy-while-wetting-his-pants.

What Lies Beneath (2000). Harrison Ford plays a professor who keeps a nasty secret from his wife, but his past comes back to, um, haunt him. Good grief, could that description *be* any more lame?

A Million Websites

Plug the word "lies" or "liars" or "lying" into your favorite search engine and you'll haul in tons of potential sites. Yet another great way to wile away the hours at work.

Before you plunge into the World Wide Web, however, here's a World Wide Warning: Any nutter with an ounce of FrontPage knowledge and a server can put up a website and post content to his heart's content. Free speech is alive and well in North America, but it ain't necessarily intelligent speech.

Best bet? Stick to the educational sites (with the *.edu* suffix) and avoid those triple-X sites like Avian Bird Flu. The relationship you save may be your own.

*It is impossible to calculate the moral mischief...
that mental lying has produced in society. When a man has
so far corrupted and prostituted the chastity of his mind as to
subscribe his professional belief to things he does not believe
he has prepared himself for the commission of
every other crime.*

— Thomas Paine
Anglo-American political theorist & writer (1737 – 1809)

Index

Was it a friend or foe that spread these lies?
Nay, who but infants question in such wise,
'Twas one of my most intimate enemies.
— Dante Gabriel Rossetti, *Fragment*
English poet and painter (1828–1882)

About The FingerTip Press

A Simple Mission from a Simple Company Run by Simple People

The FingerTip Press is proud to bring to you the *Tipping Points Digest* series — trade paperback originals, e-digests and audio digests tailor-made for time-crunched readers.

Tipping Points Digest books are written for the tired, huddled masses who are stretched to the breaking point by the competing demands of love and labor (the work, not child-bearing kind). We promise to pack our books with the freshest and funniest lifestyle and relationship tips and deliver them in the freshest and funniest formats, because nothing helps smooth over life's rough patches better than a spackle of humor. And if we make a little bit of money fulfilling our promise, we're o.k. with that, too.

But The FingerTip Press is more than just a money-grubbing publisher. (If you saw our income statements, you'd wholeheartedly agree!) We're devout believers that when it comes to our work lives and our love lives — and the stress each can impose on the other — nothing works better than humor to get us through the day. We've created two programs to help spread our gospel. We hope that after you've read about them you'll help spread the word as well!

The FingerTip Press' At-Work Attitude Adjustment Program

Businesses throughout North America and around the world are letting huge profits slip through their fingers.

Employees throughout North America and around the world are feeling more overworked and stressed than ever.

It doesn't have to be this way!

The FingerTip Press' **At-Work Attitude Adjustment** program is designed to foster a more positive attitude toward our work lives. It seeks to promote awareness among management and employees alike on the many benefits humor can bring to the workplace. It aims to dispel the myth that work isn't supposed to be fun.

Hard work doesn't have to be *that* hard!

What the Program Is *Not*

The **At-Work Attitude Adjustment** program is *not* a fee-based, consultative program.

Some companies pay "humor doctors" huge sums for keynote speeches and full-day seminars. Frankly, we believe the task of boosting humor is best left to those working within your workplace, to company insiders who know the lay of the land and the governing politics. Our program provides simple tools and simple strategies your staff can implement with ease. **Simple works.**

The **At-Work Attitude Adjustment** program is *not* about prop comedy or Andrew Dice Clay stand-up routines. We're not trying to spawn a dozen Howie Mandel clones in your office (perish the thought) or turn your customer reception area into an R-rated night club. Like we said, the program's about simple tools and simple strategies. **Simple works.**

The **At-Work Attitude Adjustment** program is *not* some half-baked, airy-fairy concept dreamed up by liberal-arts majors.

Well, not entirely.

While the publisher of The FingerTip Press does hold a Master's degree in Political Science, he has also experienced the value of humorous, stress-releasing activities first hand during his former career as a Naval Officer. If something as simple as humor can increase morale and cohesion in a warship patrolling for al-Qaeda suspects off the coast of Iran, you can bet your Argyle socks it'll help pull your marketing department together. **Simple works.**

So, what's the **At-Work Attitude Adjustment** program all about?

Simply put, it's a humor-advocacy program for fostering **positive attitudes** regarding our work lives. It seeks to **increase awareness** among management and employees alike on the urgent need to introduce more humor in the workplace — and humor's **many benefits.**

Remember the power — and profits — concealed beneath this simple equation:

More Humor = More Productivity = More Profitability

How It Works

Our At-Work Attitude Adjustment Program is simple because *simple works.* Here's what your business will receive when it becomes a member:

- The FingerTip Press offers **free, humor-boosting suggestions** at *www.tipsdigest.com,* which can be implemented by participating businesses on a daily, weekly, monthly or quarterly basis. Frequency is *your choice,* Kenneth.

- The FingerTip Press asks members to declare the first Monday in February, June and October **At-Work Attitude Adjustment Days,** days where they can rally the troops and focus them on new ways to boost workplace humor (or flog them for missing sales quotas … *your choice*).

- The FingerTip Press has a **Water Cooler** section at *www.tipsdigest.com* where members can share successful strategies for boosting workplace humor. Participation is *your choice,* but we firmly believe a few thousand heads are better than one (except when it comes to dating or haircuts).

- The FingerTip Press provides members with a PDF-format **Starter Kit.** The kit covers simple strategies for successfully implementing the program, and can be delivered electronically to any designated point-of-contact. *Your choice.*

- The FingerTip Press provides members with our monthly e-mail newsletter, ***TipsMail.*** The newsletter is tailored to assist our business members, offering them more great tips, strategies and programs for boosting humor in the workplace. It's also permission-based, so receiving it is *your choice.*

- Finally, The FingerTip Press offers members the opportunity to purchase our *Tipping Points Digest* titles at a **substantial discount,** and even provides complimentary copies to help management decide whether our digests could help positively adjust attitudes within their organization. Participation in the *Tipping Points Digest* discount program is *your choice.*

If your business, or the business you work for, could benefit from higher productivity, more creativity and more cohesive teamwork, then contact The FingerTip Press today!

It's *your choice.* (Too much with the *your choice* thing? Yeah, we thought so, too.)

The FingerTip Press' At-Home Attitude Adjustment Program

Our **At-Home Attitude Adjustment Program** reaches out to *Tipping Points Digest*'s readers to promote the relationship benefits of shared reading at home, as well as the therapeutic benefits of laughter for enhancing intimacy and reducing relationship stress.

We like to call it **The FingerTip Fifteen.**

The FingerTip Fifteen: A Prescription for What Ails Your Relationship

Driving. Working. Child rearing …

Cooking. Bill paying. Sweeping …

Vacuuming. Shaving. Sleeping …

Ever notice how 99% of the day is spent doing serious stuff, or performing tasks so routine you could do them with your eyes closed?

Ever notice how 99% of the day is spent isolated from your partner — the very person you chose to spend the rest of your life with — even when you're both in the same room?

Ever wonder where the magic went? Ever wonder if you can get it back?

The FingerTip Press is here to give the magic back to you — along with a new attitude toward your relationship.

All we ask is that you give us 1% of your day … just fifteen minutes of your time in order to reconnect with your partner. Fifteen minutes to laugh and bond — and maybe even get a little somethin' somethin'. Here's our simple prescription for curing what ails your relationship:

❖ Run, don't walk, to your favorite bookstore or specialty retailer that carries fine books. Check out *www.tipsdigest.com* for a list of *Tipping Points* Dealers near you. (If you hate running, you can order directly from the site.)

❖ Seek out our *Tipping Points Digest* titles. Look for the biggest crowd, the mob where people are tearing each others' hair out to get near the shelves. That's for the latest *Harry Potter* or *The Da Vinci Code.* We're located in the self-help or humor section. Ask the nearest employee for directions.

❖ Purchase a *Tipping Points Digest*. Be pleasantly surprised that you can still afford to pick up milk and carb-conscious bread on the way home.

❖ Run, don't walk, home with your *Tipping Points Digest*. Don't forget to pick up milk and carb-conscious bread.

❖ Choose an appropriate time to read your *Tipping Points Digest* with your partner. If we might be so bold as to make a suggestion, the perfect time might be just before you go to sleep tonight.

❖ Take your *Tipping Points Digest* to bed and spend just fifteen minutes reading it aloud with your partner. Take turns. Make up funny voices. Share the illustrations. Laugh. Cuddle. Laugh some more. And maybe, just maybe, you'll spend another fifteen minutes doing something else before you fall asleep. O.K., maybe five minutes, then.

Upcoming Titles

Coming April 2007

Blow Your Bank Wad:
More Than 101 Scandalous Ways
to Squander Your Kids' Inheritance

by Tad and Alicia Carrier-Boxmüeller

North America's Baby Boomers stand to inherit an estimated $10 trillion from their parents over the next two decades. It will represent one of the largest transfers of wealth in history.

Or at least it would have until *Blow Your Bank Wad* hit the shelves.

The husband-and-wife writing team of Tad and Alicia Carrier-Boxmüeller will captivate your imagination and kick your purchasing power into overdrive with this hilarious, thought-provoking guide to spending your progeny's cash. Here's a small sample of what you'll discover:

❖ Why you're actually doing your kids a favor by inoculating them against "affluenza"

❖ Exciting luxury destinations where you can really poach your nest egg

❖ Out-of-this-world travel that will leave you weightless

❖ To-die-for gadgets and outrageously expensive baubles for him and for her

- ❖ How to set up a revival trust and leave yourself a little something for your post-mortem re-awakening
- ❖ The bevy of fascinating TipBits and side-splitting illustrations you've come to expect from *Tipping Points Digest*

Blow Your Bank Wad will have you laughing all the way to the ATM. The kids, however, may not share your levity …

Watch for excerpts and sample chapters at
www.tipsdigest.com

Upcoming Titles

Coming November 2007

Ho-Ho-Holy Crap!:
More Than 101 Last-Minute, Relationship-Saving Gift Ideas for Holiday Procrastinators

by Richard Steven Mack

How many times has the holiday season snuck up like a stealth bomber, forcing you to buy gifts for your better half in less time than it takes to soft boil an egg?

If you're Richard Steven Mack, the answer is too many. He's learned the hard way that holiday-season procrastinators — both male and female — risk a bunker-busting bombshell in the form of an irate or hysterical partner if the prezzies don't measure up.

Rather than face each December in a panic, Mack has developed a foolproof plan of attack that will guide even the most disorganized shopper through the most frantic shopping season of the year. Here's a sample of what you'll learn in *Ho-Ho-Holy Crap!*

- Active listening skills so you can tune into the hints your partner drops year round
- The items you must have to guarantee success at the stores
- The right time of day and week to hit the malls — and when to avoid them like your hot ex

- The stores that can save your a** in an emergency
- The gifts that seem perfect, but will land you in divorce court if you dare go there
- The right and wrong ways to bribe your children to do your gift shopping

Watch for *Ho-Ho-Holy Crap!* during the 2007 holiday season … and cross *TV Guide* and AA-batteries off your gift list forever.

Visit
www.tipsdigest.com
Today!

Hack your way through the daily clutter and the daily drudgery to your computer and discover a lush oasis in the dry, dusty desert of online information.

www.tipsdigest.com is a refreshing watering hole for revitalizing your life. Think of our virtual space as your favorite pub — without the bar tabs, blackouts and raging hangovers. Like your favorite pub, *www.tipsdigest.com* is the best place to pick up the hottest … um, tips, advice and life-enhancing strategies from people who have been there, done that, and worn the freakin' t-shirt down to its last threads.

Here are six great reasons to visit *www.tipsdigest.com* today:

❖ Registration to join the *Tipster Nation!* is free.

❖ You'll receive unlimited access to self-help and how-to articles (laced with our unique brand of humor, of course!), great TipBits, awesome contests and money-saving promotions.

❖ You'll receive unlimited access to our message board, *Tipping Points of View,* where you can find and share tips, advice and success strategies with other members of the *Tipster Nation!*

❖ You'll receive terrific pre-publication offers on new *Tipping Points Digest* titles.

❖ You can sign up for *TipsMail*, our free, monthly e-mail newsletter featuring fantastic tips, excerpts from upcoming digest titles, special promotions and other must-have info not found anywhere else.

❖ You can participate in our *Tipping Points Rewards Program* and earn reward points with every purchase made from *www.tipsdigest.com*

Six great reasons to take a long, cool sip of
www.tipsdigest.com today!

You Won't Get Fooled Again:
More Than 101 Brilliant Ways
to Bust *Any* Bald-Faced Liar
(Even If the Liar is Lying Beside You!)

Do you know someone who could benefit from the bald-faced-liar busting tips featured in this digest? It's the perfect gift for any couple embarking on the long highway of togetherness, or already a few too many miles down the highway, or simply stalled on one of its many on-ramps!

Please rush me _____ copies of *You Won't Get Fooled Again* at USD$13.00/CAD$16.00 each (price includes taxes and shipping). I have enclosed a check made payable to The FingerTip Press in the amount of $________ [ ] $USD [ ] $CAD (please check one).

Full Name: ____

Address: ____

City: ________________________ State/Province: ____________

Zip/Postal Code: ____

Telephone (including area code): ___________________________

E-Mail: ____

Please allow 3–4 weeks for delivery.

Mail to:

The FingerTip Press
14 Chestnut Street, Suite 104
St. Thomas, ON N5R 2A7
Canada